HOW SEX HEALS

Collected Essays
from
Psychology Tomorrow Magazine

Special Edition

A Letter from the Editor

Sex is shrouded in such mystery and secrecy, considered so personal, that it's a wonder we can ever have an honest conversation about it. But if we could talk freely and openly with each other, we would discover that sex means something different to everyone, often far from the ideas that Hollywood and Madison Avenue feed us.

In truth, sex is not the primitive instinct that we are led to believe. It's our most complicated human need. Through sex we connect, communicate, negotiate power, give and receive pleasure, and work to heal our inner lives.

This special collection of *Psychology Tomorrow Magazine* celebrates our third anniversary of publication. It was, after all, the censorship by *Psychology Today* of one of my sex columns which led to my founding of *Psychology Tomorrow*.

These selected essays explore sex in all its complex and creative possibilities. Each article shares in common the idea that our fantasies, desires, and behaviors are windows into the deepest levels of our psyches. By understanding all of these dynamic interactions, we also come to understand our core personalities more deeply.

Further, most of our contributors – seasoned psychotherapists – believe that sex, when engaged with intention, can change our lives, help repair past conflicts, and satisfy our deepest, unmet needs. One of our authors, for instance, provides a guide for connecting the different facets of ourselves in "Sacred Sexuality and Sex," as the mind, body, and spirit unite through sex in exquisite harmony.

A few of our contributors are "sex workers" who view themselves as healers to the same extent as any therapist. For them, sex is more verb than noun. They actively focus on helping their clients understand and express their "true" needs and desires and provide the opportunity to act these out in a safe, supportive environment. The knowledge, freedom, and pleasure gained through these experiences allows their clients to achieve a level of authenticity they have rarely, if ever, experienced before.

Some essays are prescriptive. They include queries and exercises that can unlock the mysteries of our sexual fantasies, the longings underpinning our desires, the undercurrents of self-knowledge. Others simply enlighten us with their vivacious perspective.

An act which explores both hurting and healing, sex is not only a divining rod for greater self-knowledge but also serves as a reservoir of cleansing insight.

Our hope is that *How Sex Heals* will offer a new lens into your own experience with sex. One love at a time, gradually but greatly we can contribute to the slow transformation of our moralistic (yet sex-obsessed) society, one that honors the personally layered meanings and values of sex. By unveiling the mysteries of sex, we believe that we can minimize the shame and guilt so many of us ascribe to our most intimate desires, and in turn create a new societal vitality, one that reframes the erotic into a lust for compassion.

Stanley Siegel
Editor-in-Chief

Contents

How Sex Heals

by Stanley Siegel

Scientists agree that frequent sex can improve heart health, build a more robust immune system, and increase the ability to ward off pain. Sex changes brain and body chemistry, boosting certain hormone levels that keep us young and vibrant. Sex can also alter our mental state by releasing endorphins that act as antidotes to stress, anxiety, and depression.

But among the greatest miracles of sex is its most secret – its capacity to help us work through deep-seated emotional conflicts and satisfy unmet childhood needs.

The human body is designed to heal itself. We have an immune system that protects us from disease and repairs us when we are damaged. Pain acts as an alarm, alerting us to the problem. In response, all of the body's systems, including the mind, are called into action to aid in the process of self-recovery. Similarly, when we encounter emotional conflict, we also experience pain. The mind mobilizes its own defense to assist in repairing the emotional wound in the same way we release an army of antibodies to heal a cut finger. Whether it's physical or psychological, we are hard-wired to lessen pain, helped by innate mechanisms.

Among the mind's most inventive weapons in the battle for emotional recovery are our fantasies. We create them to counteract anxiety or pain, substituting pleasure where conflict exists.

As children we use imaginative play to help us gain mastery of challenging events. We try out roles as sports stars, princesses, police officers, and superheroes, enabling ourselves to feel powerful in a world in which grown-ups are in charge. In play, we find comfort often returning to the same games or stories again and again because their familiarity provides a zone in which we feel safe and increasingly competent. This same mechanism will apply later in adulthood when "playtime" occurs in the bedroom.

As we grow out of childhood and societal expectations and norms gradually restrict our imagination and behavior, we begin to apply lessons learned toward navigating the harsher realities of adult life. Yet, fantasies remain an essential part of helping us cope with life's myriad conflicts. Now we imagine being billionaires or CEO's or celebrities, rewarded with power or fame for our accomplishments, or we fantasize writing the great American novel or producing a film, becoming the pillars of our community, or simply winning the lottery. We have learned to convert painful feelings of disappointment, helplessness, failure, or loss into manageable, sometimes even pleasurable ones.

Just as fantasies of great wealth or status serve to help us feel less powerless in our ordinary lives, sexual fantasies are the mind's way of helping us gain mastery of unresolved conflicts or unmet needs. They are not simple random imaginings, as we are often led to believe. At their base lie fragments of our history that reach far back into the forgotten past. By the time we leave adolescence, most of us have eroticized some aspect of unmet needs from our childhoods, encoding them in our sexual fantasies. These encoded sexual fantasies, which continue throughout our adult lives, transform the pain associated with old wounds into sexual pleasure.

As a society, we have yet to appreciate the healing nature of sex. Instead we have a complicated relationship with sex, simultaneously promoting sexual images in popular culture – movies, television, and advertising – while demonizing those of us who enjoy it, especially women, with labels like "whore," "slut," and "player." As a consequence, many of us internalize these confusing or unrealistic messages, so by the time we reach adulthood we have no idea of what sex actually means to us. We suppress or erase our sexual desires and fantasies from our experience, if not from our consciousness altogether, creating a condition of alienation and inauthenticity – a disconnection between who we really are and how we behave. We enter a process of disengaging our minds from our bodies and souls, which often lasts a lifetime.

But if we learn to identify our sexual fantasies and true desires, where they come from and what they mean, we can unleash their full healing power. Embracing our sexual truth reverses the corrosive influences of guilt and shame, and enhances the sense of self-worth and wholeness that is essential to leading a fulfilling life. It allows us to reclaim abandoned parts of ourselves and integrate them into our being, also crucial to health. And equally important, our true desires can also become a divining rod that leads to choosing partners with whom we can build a respectful, honest, and trusting relationship, whether it is for a single night or a lifetime.

> *Whether it's physical or psychological, we are hard-wired to lessen pain, helped by innate mechanisms.*

Graceful Guidelines for Sexual Healing
by Michael Picucci

Most people in the "recovery" or "therapy" process yearn for sexual healing. I make this statement as a therapist and as a human being who has facilitated myself and many others on the journey.

Sexual healing is the shame-free revisiting of complex sexual histories, limitations, and perceptions combined with new awareness, understanding, and compassion. In this process of rejuvenation, we learn how to merge our spiritual and sexual energies. The "sexual-spiritual split" is a culturally induced, deep psychic schism that haunts relationships and precludes emotional fulfillment. Resolving this powerful inner conflict is necessary for true body, mind, and spirit connections.

These guidelines can be used to illuminate and focus a core healing journey that is central to having a mastery of life, the awareness of our aliveness, of our sensual pleasure, and of our contentment.

Five Graceful Guidelines for Sexual Healing

1. *Increase Body Awareness*
2. *Share Sexual History*
3. *Dialogue in Relationship*
4. *Create 'Fusion Exercises'*
5. *Rediscover Adolescent Awkwardness*

1. *Increase Body Awareness*

Introduce yourself to the possibility of bringing full body awareness and energy to your sexual regions. Some of us have depleted energy levels and a diminished sense of aliveness in our pelvic area and a fullness of energy in our heart region. Others feel constricted with their heart energy while having an intense pelvic charge. This is particularly evident in early intimacy and bonding. Because of this culturally fragmented energy disbursement in the body, sexual motivation usually has more to do with feelings like neediness, escape from other feelings, and proving one's self-worth, than feelings of pure pleasure and the normal desire for interconnectedness.

For many, pleasure can only be realized in highly charged scenarios. Often they are avoided because they are dangerous and/or self-destructive. Some of us are just fearfully frozen. Others become frustrated at a perceived lack of ability to negotiate the complexities. Many repeat unfulfilling patterns again and again. Whatever one's history may be, the following exercises have proven helpful in energizing and awakening sexual aliveness.

In Latin, most Eastern and metaphysical philosophies, the word "breath" is synonymous with "spirit." Conscious breathing brings energy (and spirit) into the body. This exercise will help improve anyone's ability to breathe and improve sexual aliveness. First, practice conscious, deep breathing exercises focused in the groin. Imagine that you can take your breath all the way down to the perineum, that lowermost part of the crotch between the vagina and the rectum, or the scrotum and rectum. In reality, most feel that they can't breathe into their perineum, yet imagination can produce surprising results. This exercise can be done while brushing your teeth, riding in a car, or for a few minutes before or after sleeping. While the results may not be immediate, with a little practice and patience, deeper breathing of this sort will help lead to spiritual-genital integration.

The "rotation exercise" is one that you can combine with the conscious pelvic breathing exercise. Stand up straight, put your feet shoulder-length apart, relax (unlock) your knees, and rotate your hips in a circular motion, stretching out in all directions as far as is comfortable. Imagine that you are standing in the center of a mostly empty peanut butter jar, and you want to use your hip and pelvis, in a circular motion, to clean the peanut butter off the sides of the jar. Keep rotating, first in one direction, and then the other. Lower and raise yourself to completely clean the inside of that jar.

Attention to conscious breathing will be helpful. Take a moment or two to giddily and randomly move your pelvis, tuning into the energy and spontaneously moving and following your inner current. Just go with the flow for a few moments. You will begin, subtly, at first, feeling a renewed aliveness in this region that is sensual, sexual, and centering – all at the same time.

These exercises are also excellent "warm-ups" for more pleasurable sexual experiences, alone or to be shared with a partner. (For additional information and exercises on all of the guidelines in this article see my books: *The Journey Toward Complete Recovery: Reclaiming Your Emotional and Spiritual & Sexual Wholeness* and *Ritual as Resource: Energy for Vibrant Living*.)

2. *Share Sexual History*

Begin a process of uncovering and sharing sexual secrets from your past with "safe" people. It is important to practice this with those who are sensitive, understanding, and com-

passionate listeners. These "secrets" are rightfully too sensitive to be exposed to individuals who will not endow them with suitable respect. Along with these secrets there is a need to bring awareness to religious and other spiritually infused influences on your early sexual development and evolution.

I suggest writing a narrative history, or outline, to put one's sexual development in a historical perspective. This begins with the first remembered "exposure" to sex, sexual energy, or sexual material. Then, as best you can remember, recreate your development with subsequent incidents. This exercise will help put your current sexual expression in an understandable and historical context. By sharing this history with a safe person, one can further heal the sexual-spiritual split.

After sharing "sexual histories in perspective" (in a shame-free setting), your psyche will gradually produce additional memories, further illuminating your history. Shared sexual histories provide grounding and a framework for your present experience while simultaneously creating a platform for new possibilities.

3. *Dialogue in Relationship*

Encourage yourself to risk cultivating meaningful dialogue around sexual issues in dating situations and with significant partners. The deepest interpersonal healing takes place in relationship. Finding and cultivating a safe partner is, of course, pivotal. One can do a great deal of healing with therapists and within a community. However, that healing will be limited by the appropriate professional and cultural boundaries of those relationships. To ultimately heal the sexual-spiritual split, we must explore relating to another human being while attempting to bring both polarized aspects of the split to this relationship without walls of shame arising. It is important to work through shameful aspects and feelings of inadequacy about sex with a partner. It is fine to move slowly. "Intention" and "willingness" are paramount.

4. *Create "Fusion Exercises"*

Consciously combine meditative, spiritual, or contemplative experiences with your own sexuality. Such experimentation is a very different and awkward experience for most people at first, but in time one feels a new and deeper connection with both pleasure and release. Sexual experiences often grow from being simply physical (with genital concentration), to becoming a *full-body*, kinesthetic event that can be powerful and rewarding.

Suggesting a combination of sexual and spiritual experimenting often brings laughter and confusion. People always ask, "How are we supposed to do that?" They often break out in further embarrassed laughter and disbelief when I suggest, "Try experimenting with masturbating (or self-loving) and praying at the same time!"

This laughter is a defense. Notice how foreign the suggestion feels, emphasizing the reality of an internal dichotomy! Think about this in relation to merging your core sexuality with a spiritual, loving union or relationship with yourself or another.

Create rituals with candlelight, mirrors, and incense for sessions of self-loving and self-pleasuring. Slowly begin to designate a "special time and place" in your life for, and begin to exalt in, your body (however you may perceive it), your sexuality, alone or with a companion, as an ecstatic all-encompassing manifestation of your humanity.

Use your intuitive creativity and responsible, courageous risk-taking abilities to create your own additional practices to merge sexual and spiritual energies. Like flowers growing toward the sun, as we humans experience this fusion in our psyche, our bodies and our defensive reflexes organically grow toward sexual and spiritual unity.

5. *Rediscover Adolescent Awkwardness*

Become willing to enter a period of discovery which I call "adolescent awkwardness." In dating or in a significant long-term relationship, a time comes when the healing of this internalized sexual-spiritual schism must be addressed for the relationship to grow. We must surrender preconceived concepts regarding sexuality and intimacy and join another person in authentic adolescent discovery. Many of us missed a healthy adolescence, and therefore cannot go further into intimacy without visiting this important building block. It is important to give yourself permission to feel adolescent and awkward with yourself and another. It is rich, fertile ground in which to plant seeds of new awareness. Very workable and pleasing possibilities will grow from these seeds.

Appreciate Resistance

Appreciation of our own resistance signals the most important awareness of healing. All of the above exercises will initially bring resistance to the fore. This is good: we want to bring resistance up out of the unconscious, where it has ominous rule, and expose it to a "process of resolution." By connecting with the resistance, and moving through it, we have the opportunity to discern and untangle the diverse feelings and incidents that have formed themselves into walls of shame.

Whenever shame or blockage surfaces (often feeling like a wall) in a budding or long-term intimate relationship, the struggle to share it is also the process of healthy adolescent development. It is the joining of less mature and more mature aspects of ourselves together in a sensitive, growing relationship. In this process, there is great value in the shame. Shame flirts with us. It lures us while at the same time it tries to hide. As suggested by the author Max Scheler in *Shame and Pride* (circa. 1921) "It is from in and under the shame that our *shimmering* magic emerges."

Healing is Possible:
Belief Creates the Experience

Combining love with sexual expression is an act of higher consciousness. It is important to believe that when two human beings share love's energy combined with erotic energies, a transcendent experience occurs, one that is often profoundly healing and enriching. This is a truly sacred sharing and a goal of a fulfilling sexual experience. Reaching this goal is the result of a conscious *give and take*, a negotiation of openhearted interconnectedness. Accepting that this is awkward, we need to learn to communicate our needs, desires, fantasies and fears. Under each of the three currents are powerful and subtle feelings and energies that want to be expressed.

Releasing these expressions helps us grow holistically; they teach us about natural ag-

gression and passivity, about our feminine and masculine energies, and about pleasuring and being pleasured. They help to dissolve shame, insecurities, and to accept contradictions and complexities. They expose the need to experience them fully for healing, growth, and in understanding ourselves.

It is fine to move slowly. "Intention" and "willingness" are paramount.

Contrary to what some believe about healthy sexuality, we need to learn that healthy loving expression includes the expression of our more shadowy desires as well as our tenderness. The delicate opening up of our repressed sexual histories, variations, deviations, and fantasies is enriching as well as healing. True and spiritual love-making is the interweaving choreography of our higher and shadow selves. A holistic experience involves bringing together aspects of higher and lower self — how beautiful, and so very intimate to do so with open hearts.

Evaluating Our Progress

To evaluate your progress in healing the sexual-spiritual split, I encourage you to simply ask yourself: What motives do I bring to sexuality? What do I want from the sexual aspect of my nature?

You will know that the healing is progressing when the answers to these questions emphasize spiritual fulfillment, integrating aggression and passivity, power and surrender, femininity and masculinity, the desire for personal and shared experiences of fulfillment, pleasure, and higher consciousness.

What Brings You To Orgasm?

by Stanley Siegel

It's really what you *THINK*.

Question whether you might believe sex to be primal or complicated, prescribed or explored, destined or deviant, or anywhere along any of these spectrums. Where we land may help to elucidate how we give and receive pleasure, negotiate our interpersonal proclivities, and even more daringly how we connect and communicate with our self.

Sexual fantasies are a nearly universal experience. Whether they are a long, drawn-out story or a quick flash of imagery, they have the purpose of arousing us. Sometimes we may not be fully conscious that we are being aroused, but when we are, it's likely to lead to some form of sexual activity, from masturbation to intercourse.

But what many of us don't recognize (or if we do, are fearful to acknowledge) is that what we are actually engaging in physically with a partner may be less compelling than what goes on in our private thoughts and fantasies at the time. In fact, for most of us, it is more often the images, thoughts, and fantasies in our imagination during sexual contact that bring us closer to climax. In other words, what gets us off is what we are fantasizing.

Why? Because for the vast majority of us, our deepest sexual desires originate from unresolved conflicts or unmet needs, and our sexual fantasies represent the stories we tell ourselves to solve these issues and conflicts.

As human beings we are naturally driven toward self-healing, whether it's a small cut on our skin or deep psychological trauma. Rather than becoming defeated by feelings of isolation, helplessness, invisibility, loneliness, or rejection, carried from childhood, our mind creates fantasies turning painful feelings into pleasurable ones by allowing us to become aroused by them.

The themes that we have eroticized in our fantasies are windows into the deepest levels of our psyches. At their base lie fragments of our history, conflict, and strife that reach far back into the forgotten past. By understanding them, we not only come to understand our basic personalities, we can also learn to use to use them to create greater authenticity and intimacy in our lives.

For many of us, our fantasies remain hidden from our awareness or seem vague and ambiguous. When we are conscious of them, they are often shadowed by shame; we tend to think of them as deviant, perverse, or sinful because we do not understand their significance and instead internalize how powerful institutions such as religion and psychology have defined them. We police, deny, suppress, or keep our erotic lives secret. In the process, we disown an important part of who we are and who we could become.

In fact, no agreement exists among mental health professionals regarding what type of fantasy should be considered "healthy." Freud and other early psychoanalysts believed that sexual fantasies resulted from feelings of deprivation experienced in the absence of sexual satisfaction. Many experts still maintain this point of view and further reason that certain types of fantasies are signs of psychopathology. A fantasy involving a patient's sexual submissiveness, for instance, is seen as a deeper symptom of "masochism" rather than, as I came to see it, our mind's attempt to master unresolved, deep-seated power issues.

Where some schools of psychology tend to treat fantasies as pathological, many religious groups preach that sexual fantasies are sinful and strictly prohibited by the Bible, particularly those that involve a partner other than a spouse. Both systems of thinking have contributed to our feelings of sexual shame and confusion and have led to a cultural epidemic of sexual dysfunctions. It's the rare person who can turn off their fantasies at the suggestion of a therapist or clergymen. Doesn't understanding their meaning and purpose make more sense?

This step of what I call *Intelligent Lust*, the process by which we come to conceptualize and understand our deepest sexual desires, is called "Identifying Fantasies and True Desires," which helps us to pinpoint the themes of our fantasies and author them into words and stories. Many of us are not entirely conscious of exactly what our fantasies are. They may seem too abstract or ephemeral to follow; we may have to work hard to retrieve them from our subconscious imagination.

Fantasies and Gender

Research has shown that fantasies differ along gender lines. In general, because of many social influences and deep cultural training, men and women tend to think about sex differently. Women more commonly connect sex with love, while men more frequently detach sex from affection and experience it as recreational. Men's fantasies tend to objectify people and emphasize body parts, while women's fantasies tend toward mystery, seduction, and romantic themes, many of which are forced upon us by the media. Studies suggest that male fantasies tend to be shorter and imagistic, while female fantasies tend to have more narrative as well as greater focus on the relationship between characters in the fantasy. The essence of a male fantasy might be captured in a few seconds-long photographic clips, while a female's fantasy might amount to an entire film. Women's stories tend to have smell and sound effects.

Studies suggest that male fantasies tend to be shorter and imagistic, while women's fantasies tend to have more narrative as well as a greater focus on the relationship between the characters in the fantasy.

Interestingly, there appears to be little difference in fantasies based on sexual orientation as it relates to gender; that is, heterosexual and homosexual men tend to focus on specific body parts and casual sexual encounters, while straight and lesbian women's fantasies contain more emotion and affection. It's also not uncommon for men and women who identify as heterosexual to sometimes become aroused by fantasies of same-sex partners. Data gathered through self-report show this to be considerably more common with women.

Yet such numbers may not portray an accurate picture of the situation, since it has also been shown that men are more likely to fear being labeled as "queer" and consequently to minimize and under-report past or present sexual fantasies involving other men. But even though there are general themes related to gender, the details of our sexual fantasies are primarily based on each of our personal histories and psychologies.

To get in the right frame of mind, you should start to ask yourself and answer questions that will help you identify the key elements that make up your fantasies. By asking yourself these questions, the themes and narratives of your fantasies come into focus. Language has a way of making fantasies real.

Once we put thoughts and images into words and sentences, we tend to own them more completely. Take the time to think deeply about your answers to these questions. Write them down if possible. Your erotic images and thoughts may surprise or even frighten you, but keep in mind that they all have unique meanings which you will learn to understand.

Inside Your Fantasies

- What do you think about during sex?
- Is there a central or main fantasy?
- What mental image or thought actually brings you to climax?
- What is the specific plot or story line in your fantasies?
- Do you think about sex with people other than your partner? Past partners or strangers?

- How would you describe the characters in your fantasy?
- What action are you taking in your fantasy?
- How are other people acting toward you?
- What is your attitude in the fantasy? What is the attitude of the other person(s) involved?
- What sexual thoughts do you have that embarrass you?
- What sexual feelings bring you shame or guilt?
- What are you thinking about when you can't climax?
- What fantasies have you already acted out? What was the result?
- Have you had a sexual experience that you continue to fantasize about? What in particular was so exciting about the experience?
- Do your sexual fantasies include force?
- Do you focus on body parts such as breasts or penises? Which ones?
- Are articles of clothing such as shoes, leather, scarves, or lingerie part of your fantasy? How are they used?
- What do you think about when you're having sex with a partner?

Making Sex Positive Choices

by Stanley Siegel

Most of us, gay and straight alike, feel that having a lifelong partner is preferable to going through life alone or with a series of affairs or short-term relationships. There is much in our culture that supports this notion, from the large number of tax benefits given to married couples, to the countless themes of Sunday morning church services. And while we idealize this idea in movies, television shows, novels, and fairy tales, forging a successful long-term relationship is quite another story.

Statistics over the last few decades show that nearly half of all marriages end in divorce, though the number has been decreasing slightly in recent years. Among the most commonly reported reasons are problems related to sex, especially the loss of intimacy and infidelity. Yet we still underestimate the importance of sex in our relationships, placing it low on the list of priorities. Collectively, we fail to appreciate sex as a spiritual and psychological affirmation of life.

Smart sex requires understanding and exploring our true sexuality openly and responsibly without presuppositions. The process better prepares us for the issues that typically occur in relationships because, through sex, we communicate intimately, negotiate power, give and receive pleasure, and sometimes heal our past. The act of giving and receiving pleasure can make facing life's daily challenges much easier. By making sexual fulfillment a prominent part of our relationships and giving it greater importance, we are less likely to fight over folding the laundry or the details of renovating a house. No matter what struggles we face, we momentarily put them aside and establish a time and place to embrace intimacy and desire.

Whether it's because of an absence of communication or misunderstanding of our true desires, problems arise when our thoughts and feelings go unspoken; sexual frustration and resentment builds. The key to the longevity of relationships is in maintaining an ongoing conversation even when it's difficult – at times when we lose sexual interest in a partner, fantasize about less conventional sex, or feel sexually interested in other people. When these feelings do occur, it's essential to acknowledge them to each other and make an intelligent decision about what to do, rather than keeping them secret or sweeping them under the rug.

It's secrecy that threatens the relationship because, in hiding our desires, we often subvert feelings into self-serving, abusive, or manipulative behavior.

Instead, we must consider all the possible solutions, from finding a way to bring sex back into the relationship, to polyamory – consistent sex with multiple partners – in order to remain genuinely invested in the authenticity and integrity of the relationship. It's not monogamy that necessarily improves the chances of a relationship's survival; rather, it's our ability to confront the truth about our desires and navigate all the possibilities for their fulfillment that will lead to greater understanding and connection.

Under these circumstances, monogamy should be equally considered along with consensual alternatives; a conscious choice should be made based on what feels right for the individuals involved.

My patients Paul and Melissa found a happy middle ground to deal with their sexual differences, while Margot and Billy broke conventional boundaries. Both couples dared to make sex a vital part of their lives, a rich fertile ground in which to cultivate deep self-knowledge and true acceptance.

Paul, my patient, is an older man who has been married three times; Melissa, twenty years younger, has never been married and has tended to bounce from one relationship to the next. They met when fixed up by a friend, and hit it off immediately.

In the past, both Paul and Melissa had dated perfectionists whom they felt a strong need to please based on similar childhood experiences with equally demanding parents. Eventually, they always rebelled against their partners' demands, and all their relationships ended in failure – a common trait they discovered on their first date, and one they liked talking about, as now they had each found a partner whom they didn't feel the need to please, as much as simply enjoy. As neither had many expectations of the other, they felt no need to protest and in a short time grew quite close.

Not long into their relationship, Paul and Melissa came to me for couples counseling. They wanted their relationship to work out, but were concerned because the sex hadn't been good. It quickly became clear that despite their ability to discuss almost anything, they hadn't been talking to each other about sex; they had only been fumbling around unhappily in bed. Over time, I took them through the steps, opening their minds to what they truly wanted from sex, investigating their fantasies, talking candidly as much as felt comfortable for them.

It's secrecy that threatens relationships because, in hiding our desires, we often subvert feelings into self-serving, abusive, or manipulative behaviors.

What they discovered was that, at sixty-seven, Paul's sexual drive was a fraction of what it had been. He was growing to love Melissa, but much of that came from her companionship and the close physical contact they both enjoyed.

Melissa, twenty years younger, however, was still sexual. Because her fantasies often centered on being told what to do by an authoritarian man, the couple eventually developed a practice that satisfied both of them: In bed, Paul would hold Melissa and tell her exactly what she should do to reach orgasm on her own. Once she had, Melissa would take time to embrace and caress Paul, which pleased him immensely.

This might strike some people as an odd compromise, but it was anything but that to the couple, who could now not only talk about sex but could also regularly embellish on the scene to make it uniquely theirs – and it made them very happy as well.

Like most couples, Margot and Billy had married without much discussion of sex. For the two years since, both imagined the other enjoyed their love making, though privately each felt detached and unsatisfied. They cared about each other deeply, got along well in most ways, and shared similar values about life. But without honest communication about sex, which each withheld for fear of upsetting the other, they had grown quietly more distant.

When Margot, with my encouragement, finally asked Billy if they could talk about their sex lives, he actually felt relieved. Since then, they've had regular conversations in which they followed the steps of *Intelligent Lust*. Each had come to recognize what he/she had eroticized earlier in their lives as well as the meaning behind those desires.

Margot's mother was a ballet dancer who retired after a knee injury. She had pinned her hopes on her only daughter, pushing her into ballet class and local performances at an early age. She called on Margot, who was by nature shy and reluctant, at every social occasion to dance for friends and family. "Frankly," Margot told me, "I had no talent and no interest, but that never stopped my mother. She was determined for me to be the star she never was."

By the time Margot reached adolescence, she resented both dance and her mother's control.

Despite these feelings, she began daydreaming about performing for school friends and boys from the neighborhood. She had read the story of Salome for a school project and imagined herself as the beautiful seductress, dancing with her seven veils.

Gradually, her daydreams became sexual fantasies in which she imagined herself dancing naked in front of men. Without knowing it, she had eroticized the painful feelings that surrounded her mother's demands, bringing instead deep pleasure to the very thing she feared and hated. As she grew into adulthood, the majority of her masturbatory fantasies focused on having sex while being watched. Yet, because these fantasies also felt as if she were surrendering to her mother, she made a decision to avoid sex altogether and therefore rarely engaged in it.

"No one would know it," Margot said to me early in our therapy. "If I would let myself go, I would be a full-blown exhibitionist!"

Billy, on the other hand, felt invisible as a child. He was the middle of five siblings and while he wasn't neglected, he did feel overlooked. A shy boy, Billy was small for his age and didn't mature as rapidly as his brother or peers at school.

One day when he was fourteen, he walked in on his older brother having sex with his girlfriend. From that time on, Billy couldn't get the images out of his thoughts. Soon he began masturbating imagining other people having sex, never picturing himself engaging in it. He was always the observer. In his unconscious mind, he had merged the episode with his brother with childhood feelings of invisibility and from that crucible, created an erotic fantasy that brought pleasure to what had caused unhappiness and confusion.

They were, after all, betraying the social conventions with which they were raised.

Now, as an adult, his sexuality was dependent on not being seen or actually participating in sex, a secret which kept him emotionally and sexually distant from Margot. That was, until they began speaking about it with my encouragement.

Instead of feeling threatened, the honesty of these conversations had sparked a sense of discovery and excitement. When Margot finally shared her fantasies with Billy, and that she imagined performing sexually for an audience of men, he laughed rather expressing outrage as she expected. He immediately confessed that he shared her fantasy and had been secretly imagining her with other men as a way of climaxing on the rare occasions they had sex. Rather than dividing them, the conversations brought them emotionally closer and soon they started discussing how they could act out their mutual fantasies safely.

When Margot finally suggested they visit a sex club, Billy jumped at the idea and together they searched the Internet. They decided on a club in another city because there would be less chance of running into anyone they knew. They planned a weekend away and agreed to a series of ground rules for how they would conduct themselves at the club, even creating a discrete "stop signal," a tug to the earlobe, to signal his/her discomfort with anything that happened.

Going to the sex club was enormously exciting, though not without anxiety. They were, after all, betraying the social conventions with which they were raised.

Checking their clothing at the door, they entered a room full of other couples engaged in various forms of sex. The freedom to be sexual in a public place, or in Billy's case to watch people acting sexual, was immediately liberating and thrilling for both of them. With Billy's consent, Margot eventually joined in and like Salome, teased and seduced a group of men and women. Amazingly, Billy felt no jealousy. In fact, he experienced Margot's behavior as an act of love and generosity, which turned him on sexually even more. No one had ever placed his needs first, and while he knew she was satisfying her own as well, for the first time in his life, he ironically felt "seen."

For weeks after, they discussed their feelings about the experience. The act of expressing their erotic fantasies by transgressing sexual convention opened up conversations about trust, jealousy, rivalry, boundaries, and limits, further deepening the intimacy and bond between them. Where Margot had always felt controlled and disrespected by her mother, she now felt profoundly appreciated and respected by the person who mattered most in her life.

Margot and Billy had the courage to break tradition – the family and social rules with which they were raised – and invent an original relationship in which they honored powerful longings and desires, giving pleasure to themselves and each other as well as depth and substance to their lives.

What Your Favorite Porn Says About You

by Stanley Siegel

You are sitting in front of a computer screen surfing porn sites, ready to get off. You sift through scenes and images until you connect to one. Suddenly, every element of desire falls perfectly in line. You become intensely excited, your physical and mental energy sharply focused, shutting out other thoughts. Eventually, you climax.

Most of us do not meticulously analyze what just happened. There might be some curiosity about why a certain porn scene turns us on. Typically, after getting off to it, we feel temporarily satisfied and pull ourselves back together.

What actually is happening in that moment when everything clicks? Why does a particular story or scene cause such arousal? Why, for instance, does forced sex with a woman or a very boyish man attract us more than other images?

Sexual fantasies, whether comprised of elaborate romantic themes or sporadic images of muscular arms or big breasts, mean much more than we think. Specific erotic images are connections to deeper inner truths long banished from our consciousness.

Porn intensely focuses our mental and physical attention, uncovering specific emotions eroticized much earlier in life. Through our sexual fantasies, we attempt to master feelings of powerlessness, shame, guilt, fear, and loneliness that have followed us into adulthood. Encoded in the porn scenes that lead us to orgasm are the psychological antidotes to these feelings. Situating ourselves in humiliating, romantic or risky scenes counteracts painful feelings by turning them into pleasurable ones. Psychologically, this happens outside our awareness, the way blood cells heal a cut finger without our knowing it.

To decode eroticized feelings, look at family dynamics. Childhood conflicts produce strong emotions that never completely disappear. Their impact echoes long into adulthood, woven into our fantasies, even when denied. What arouses us is far from random or meaningless. The porn we choose to watch is dictated by our psychological histories.

So, as you continue to read, consider your answers to these questions as you think about the porn you watch:

- What was your scariest experience growing up?
- Were you afraid of your parents?
- When did you not feel accepted or ignored by a parent, sibling or friend?
- When did you feel controlled by your parents?
- Could you discuss anger with them or disagree with them?
- Were you regularly spanked or disciplined as a child?

The basic question to put to yourself is this one: How is the feeling in your favorite porn video like the feeling you had during a conflict in your childhood?

Suppose our parents, teachers, or clergy used excessive shame or guilt to teach or control us. To deal with our resultant anger, we encode the shame in our fantasies, becoming aroused when thinking of ourselves as naughty or engaging in secret or forbidden sexual acts. We feel excited, for example, when punished or disciplined for supposed misbehavior, by being tied up and forced to have sex. Forced to surrender sexually to a dominant aggressor, we allow ourselves to enjoy the sex while escaping from the guilt that has haunted us through life.

On the other hand, some of us respond to underlying guilt and shame by sexualizing the idea of becoming the aggressor, perhaps delving into themes of incest or other extreme sexual behaviors to attach pleasure to unthinkable acts.

As children our sense of self-worth largely depends on how our parents hold and value us as distinct persons separate from the experiences they underwent. Our self-esteem, sense of competence, and ability to cope in the world is shaped by specific family dynamics.

Frequent interactions defined by negativity and disparaging comparisons leave us with deep feelings of inadequacy and, most harmfully, a notion of not being lovable. Whether we accept failure as inevitable or rebel against it and become an overachiever, that lack of self-worth influences all our interactions with the world.

It can also define our sexuality. Eroticizing feelings of inadequacy leads to fantasies with themes involving submission, humiliation, verbal abuse, or extreme adoration of a partner. We are aroused by being treated as if we are useless, unworthy, or weak. Yet, by inviting our own humiliation, we take charge of it and, through the sexual pleasure we receive, it weakens the impact of our childhood pain.

Some of us, on the other hand, counteract feelings of inadequacy with ideas of grandiosity in which we imagine ourselves as important, powerful, or irresistibly sexy. We invent fantasies in which we are admired, adored,

paid for sex, recreating ourselves as competent, powerful, and unattainable.

The most common feelings people eroticize are:

- Powerlessness and helplessness.
- Detachment and emptiness.
- Rejection and abandonment.
- Anger and aggression.
- Inadequacy, guilt, and shame.
- Insecurity, loneliness and vulnerability.

Two recent cases from my practice illustrate what I mean. In my patient Laura's family, any sexual reference was totally frowned upon. When she was a toddler, Laura's father abandoned her, her sister, and her mother Edna for another woman. Over the following years, Edna grew increasingly protective of her daughters. Fearing they would suffer her fate, Edna raised her daughters to believe that all men are unfaithful. "Even my father had cheated on my mother," Edna repeatedly told them.

Edna forbade the girls to attend school dances and demanded extra homework time, watching over them like a hawk. Academic excellence, she insisted, guaranteed independence from a man. Laura obeyed and did very well in school. Her mother was actually pleased Laura was shy and socially awkward with boys.

Yet by high school, when Laura began to have sexual feelings, she often had the same fantasy. Her mother had warned her: "Boys took advantage of me sexually." That very idea excited Laura. "I would imagine one boy in particular. He was known as a stud. He would force sex on me. I'd resist, but he would eventually overpower me and fuck me,"

Laura told me. This theme became the center of her erotic thoughts and behavior. As a young adult, she masturbated to videos featuring such men. Submerged in her moments of pleasure, though, lay Laura's conflicted past.

*   *   *

As a gay man, Stephen was comfortable with his sexuality. He regularly dated and had sex. When he climaxed, he noted that his thoughts frequently had drifted to a particular porno scene that had fixated him since he was a teen: humiliation scenes. So, Stephen fantasized being on his knees in front of another man, begging for sex. He also imagined the man spitting on him as both a "humiliation and a gift." Because he felt ashamed of these desires, he never shared them with partners, nor sought them out in sexual encounters. He satisfied them by watching porn.

In his childhood, to relieve her loneliness, Stephen's mother turned him into her confidant. With his father regularly gone on business, Stephen was often home with only his sister and mother. Stephen did not miss his father because they were ill at ease with each other.

Since childhood, Stephen knew his femininity made his father uncomfortable, as he'd tried to change Stephen by forcing him to play sports and "act like a boy." Despite his mother's interventions, his father prevailed.

Not surprisingly, Stephen never felt he measured up to his father's expectations. But rather than surrendering, Stephen grew defi-

ant. In early adolescence he declared his sexuality, making his father even angrier.

Despite fighting his father's contempt, the years of paternal denigration had seeped into Stephen's consciousness. Not only had he internalized the shame, he had eroticized it. "I fantasized being humiliated. But I took things one step further. By being humiliated through sex, at least I could feel good too," Stephen acknowledged.

*   *   *

Porn is a window into the deepest levels of your psyche. From it you can discover your deepest desires, where they come from and what they mean. The next time you find yourself enjoying your favorite porn scene, take a moment to think about the feelings that got you off and the possible history behind it.

Yet, by inviting our own humiliation, we take charge of it and, through the sexual pleasure we receive, it weakens the impact of childhood pain.

This may seem like a heavy task. It might even feel like it will spoil your fun. But understanding the psychological imprinting that shapes your desires will show what conflicts or unmet needs still require resolution. That knowledge can lead you to a more authentic sex life with your current partner or guide you in choosing a partner with whom you are sexually and otherwise compatible.

Here is a list of some more questions to help you establish the link between your favorite porn and the family conflict or unmet need that has shaped your desire:

- What is the specific story line in your favorite porn?
- How would you describe the characters' attitudes and feelings in the video?
- Which character do you identify with?
- How does that character's behavior excite you?
- Is there a specific image, or body part that gets you off?
- When in the past did you experience the feelings you've identified?
- What were the circumstances and the people in that experience?

- Was this a one-time conflict or ongoing one?
- Did the feelings change over time?
- Do you feel afraid of your own anger?
- Were there events that lead to dramatic changes in family life?
- What were your reactions to the change?
- How did family members handle your feelings at the time?
- What emotional need do you feel was not satisfied during your childhood?
- What is your most basic emotional need now?

In Favor of Casual Sex

by Stanley Siegel

Every sexual experience represents a moment of extreme intensity in which our entire inner life, our history and imagination, is expressed in action. It's an altered state of consciousness in which the past and present, body, mind, and spirit all merge to form a new reality unlike any other experience in our lives. It is impossible for any sexual experience to be absent of emotion or even to lack meaning. Even when we feel emotionally detached during sex, we aren't really devoid of emotion. Looked at more deeply, such apparent detachment is in fact a reflection of emptiness that we may feel more generally in our lives.

To understand the truth about our individual sexuality, it's important to first challenge conventional beliefs and values. What lies under many accepted "truths" about sex are in fact deeply entrenched myths that confuse rather than enlighten us. By accepting these myths at face value, we close off opportunities to explore and express the originality of our individual desires.

Among the greatest myths is that sexual intimacy can only exist within marriage or a committed long-term relationship, an idea that has entered into popular culture in the form of the ultimate prescription for happiness. How many times have you heard marriage advocates cite research purportedly showing that spouses are happier than single people or its corollary, single people are "damaged" by their fear of commitment?

But long-term relationships or marriage do not guarantee a satisfying emotional life or sexual intimacy. Everyone knows someone stuck in a barren marriage, whose members have lost their autonomy and in which sex has disappeared. Despite this, many of us still cling to the belief that sexual fulfillment and happiness can only be found through commitment. As a culture, we refuse to consider any alternatives to traditional relationships as meaningful or valid.

Yet those of us, like myself, who embrace casual sex and short-term relationships as an alternative know that, under the right circumstance, they can be deeply satisfying and meaningful choices far from devoid of depth or emotion, and sometimes more intimate than a long-term relationship.

Upon turning sixty-five, I recognized that in casual sex I'd even achieved levels of intimacy that were more transformative than in the two long-term relationships I have had. Unencumbered by a complex commitment, the freedom found in casual sex allowed me to move beyond self-consciousness to attain a degree of honesty and authenticity for myself, and my partner, in a way previously unknown to me.

With each new experience, the process of discovering and sharing specific sexual interests required verbal and non-verbal communication that was intensely focused and rapidly telegraphed. Self-disclosure and vulnerability were as necessary a part of these exchanges as they were in a committed relationship.

In fact, my experience runs contrary to the belief that commitment and intimacy need to be sustained to be meaningful. Over the course of one evening, I have shared extraordinary tenderness, generosity, and affection. Knowing that it would end shortly did not lessen my commitment to these values. Instead, it intensified them.

By openly exploring my fantasies and true desires with different partners in a way that was not possible in my committed relationship, I was often able to transcend inhibitions. With each new encounter I discovered and expressed buried parts of myself and, in time, experienced much of who I am sexually and otherwise. I have even had profound, revelatory moments that unraveled the past and showed me things I never knew about myself. I have satisfied unmet needs by embracing those aspects of my sexuality that were deeply buried and, over time, I have let some fantasies go because, having fulfilled them in reality, they no longer carry importance.

Some casual encounters presented the unexpected, both splendid and repellent. Some led to love affairs, others to friendships. Together, these experiences offered insights into the deepest levels of my psyche that have been as rich and transforming as any epiphany I have had during my long-term relationships. My sense of security and self-confidence was strengthened as I learned to negotiate all forms of rejection and rejecting someone with whom I was not sexual compatible. And I continue to refine my own moral compass based on the respect, trust, honesty and generosity I have experienced through these encounters rather than on social or religious rules.

Opponents of casual sex say it is reckless. Casual sex spreads diseases. But it isn't casual sex that spreads disease, it's unsafe sex that does. Medicine has taught us how to effectively avoid sexually transmitted diseases. Reckless behavior can certainly happen during casual sex (though there is nothing inherently reckless about it) when a partner's actions are self-centered or abusive or driven by substance abuse. We teach our sons and daughters to feel suspicious, guilty and shameful about sex, and cloak it in such mystery and secrecy that many of us have no framework for navigating sex with openness, appreciation, and grace. We can only express our true sexual desires if we are intoxicated and do not have to take responsibility for them.

On the other hand, when we do honor and embrace our individual sexuality we can be free to experience its deeper nature and to choose partners with whom we are sexually compatible, and who help us explore the truth of who we are as sexual beings. Under such conditions, sex is not something one person does to another, nor is it a guessing game.

Instead, we become like veteran artists. Our tastes and inventiveness grow more nuanced with time, as does our capacity to support different partners' sexual truths. Through the diversity of experiences found in casual sex, we can discover or reclaim parts of ourselves that have been unknown or forgotten. Fully embracing our sexuality is not a static process, as our desires slowly unfold over the course of our lifetimes. As we continue to explore who we are through sex, new desires or preferences will surface when we no longer require the old ones. We sublimely discover many truths.

Engaging in casual sexual experiences can also help us decide what we need at various points in our lives. What does become clear is that whether we believe that being single or married will bring us fulfillment, sexual compatibility should be a high priority. Some of my patients have met their long-term partners after having a casual sexual experience with them in which they discovered, among other things, that they shared similar sexual interests.

Casual sex can be smart sex, and smart sex is responsible sex. It involves self-knowledge, self-esteem, and respect for our partners. We can use casual sex intelligently to learn to honor and accept who we are, heal the consequences of shame and guilt, and celebrate the importance of sex as a positive force in our lives.

My Father the Ethical Slut

by Alyssa Siegel

Like my father, the Editor-in-Chief of *Psychology Tomorrow Magazine*, I am a psychotherapist. We both specialize in sex. In our unique personal and professional relationship, we agree on many things. However, some of our opinions and practices diverge.

It's common knowledge that teens tend to rebel against their parents' wisdom and mandates. So imagine this:

Rather than having a father who towers above you, warning about the risks of sex, instilling fear about pregnancy, disease, and the predatory nature of boys who only use you for it, who rather than judging and guarding your development to determine whether or not you have become sexually active, instead asks if you feel you are ready and if you have any questions, then hands you some condoms and tells you to have fun.

What would you do?

Well, most people would probably answer that they would do just that. Have fun. Experiment. Maybe even go a little crazy.

But not me. Oh, no.

That's not to say that I didn't start having sex in my teen years. It's just that I looked at my free pass, my dance card, with skepticism. Hesitation. If my parents weren't going to guard my sacred virginity like a lion at the gate, then I guess it was my responsibility to make a decision about what I wanted to do with it.

Still, it wasn't long before I did, of course, decide to try it out. And as it is for many people, that first time was nothing particularly special, physically or otherwise. It was painful, awkward, uncomfortable. It was not re-

markably loving or tender, but I don't think that I was expecting it would be. It was a growth experience like any other, no more and no less. It was a way in which I learned new things about myself, how both my body and mind responded to engaging in a new kind of way. It didn't greatly affect my identity nor did it in any way influence my self-esteem. It wasn't something that I started to use to get others to like me. All in all, I would say, it was a pretty healthy way to enter into this new world of sexuality. It could probably have been better. But it also definitely could have been worse.

Over those first few months of sexual activity, I gradually shared what I was feeling with my father. Throughout, he remained open and non-judgmental, turning questions back to me so that I might search my heart and find my own wisdom to process my experiences. The one thing that I know that my father still regrets was that while he was careful to ask me about whether I felt I was ready to become sexually active, he did not ask whether I believed my chosen partner was as well.

And not surprisingly, before long, the boy I was seeing did end our relationship, though not before starting a new one. And, of course, I was devastated, but no more so than any other young person who thought they were in love would be. And this was how I learned that choosing to share yourself sexually with someone is a two-part deal. It's about knowing yourself, who you really are, what you really want, what your limits are, and knowing your partner well enough to know that they have done the same and are up to the task of being honest about it.

The thing about sex is that, for kids, it's not a matter of *if*. It's a matter of *when, why, how* and with *whom*. My father's approach to my sexual curiosity and development was far from being irresponsible. My development was informed and empowering. But it was also different than what I knew to be the approach of my friends' parents.

So here's how it all turned out. Starting around age 15, I became a serial monogamist. I had sex, I enjoyed sex, but only within the context of a long-term relationship and with someone I trusted and knew well. I didn't have one-night stands or sex with a partner with whom I was not romantically involved. Many years later, immediately following my divorce, my relationships tended to get whittled down from a few years to a few months for a period of time, but the structure was essentially the same.

Now I am in a partnership that I see being a lifelong commitment. And I see it remaining monogamous.

My father writes often about non-monogamy and about casual sex and the benefits associated with both. His article *In Defense of Casual Sex* even went viral.

I really respect and admire his position, but casual sex just doesn't work for me. I used to wish it would. I have even seen that as a setback and a weakness in myself. But inevitably I have returned to the same conclusion: It doesn't work for me.

Everyone's psychological makeup is different. It is impossible to precisely conclude why we are who we are and why we choose the way we do based on every event and interaction in our histories. The best we can do is to make connections and find themes. A theme

for my father is that some of his most intimate and meaningful sexual encounters have been brief and with people whom he knew just casually.

I presume that is because his authenticity allows him the freedom to have such sex. For me, I find that I cannot open up and feel present enough in my body to experience sexual pleasure with someone whom I don't feel close to beyond physical attraction. I don't know why this is; I'm not sure that it matters.

In both our cases, we are acting in a way that works. A way that is genuine and intentional. Part of the reason why my father's ideas are so overwhelmingly popular, striking a chord for so many, is because he presents an argument that is counter to the norm. But the norm is typically a place where you don't find a whole lot of thoughtful insight and intentional choice.

So while my sexual personality and preferences are more traditional, more indicative of the historic norm, it doesn't come from a puritanical place ruled by fear or condemnation. It doesn't come from a place of conformity, to maintain the status quo, to prevent societal chaos. It comes from me. My comfort level. My knowledge of myself, based on my own, lived, personal experiences.

If I were queen of the world (a common fantasy of mine), I would encourage everyone to follow their own hearts and refrain from condemning others for doing the same. This is an ideology that I wholeheartedly and consistently bring into my work with clients. It's not about when and with whom you choose to have sex, it's that you keep it honest, keep the communication open, and make choices from a place of self-awareness and respect. Not only will it result in a happier and more satisfying life, it's a hell of a lot easier.

Should We Have Sex Just Because Our Partner Wants To?

by Neil McArthur

The Telegraph recently reported that a man in France has been fined the equivalent of $14,000 for refusing to have sex with his wife…for 21 years. The man said he was tired and hadn't been feeling that well. For twenty-one years. I'm not kidding. The judge didn't buy it either. He said: "By getting married, couples agree to sharing their life and this clearly implies they will have sex with each other."

Maybe you have to be French to think that being denied sex is a reason to actually take your partner to court, but the case brings up a profound moral question: Do we have an obligation to try to satisfy our partners when it comes to sex?

What the experts call "desire discrepancy" – when one partner wants sex a lot more than the other one does – is something that a very large number of couples face. Therapists say it is the most common sexual problem they deal with, and while we don't have good statistics on it, some experts have estimated that as many as one in three couples will confront it at some point.

There is even a medical term, "hypoactive sexual desire disorder" (HSDD), for people, mostly women, who experience low levels of sexual desire. Twenty percent of people are thought to be suffering from HSDD. And someone can be diagnosed with HSDD if they have normal levels of desire overall, but are just not attracted to their current partner. Of course, the quest is under way for a drug, as Daniel Bergner chronicled in a fascinating piece for the New York Times.

Luckily, there's a non-pharmaceutical solution to the problem of desire discrepancy that's also cheap and available without a prescription, and that works immediately.

Here it is: Have sex.

* * *

Like everything in life, there are advantages and disadvantages to this treatment. On the down side, it means you have to clear some time in your schedule, put off that "House of Cards" marathon, and let that stack of unread New Yorkers get that much higher. (Those things never stop coming!)

On the upside, you get to have more sex. And at least one study has suggested that you'll be happier overall. According to a 2012 paper in The Journal of Sex Research, which Debby Herbenick wrote about for Salon, "Women and men reported higher levels of relationship satisfaction when their partners said they'd made more 'sexual transformations,'" – including more frequent sex.

In other words, relationship sex is a bit like going out dancing on a Saturday night in February. It's easy to think you'd rather just spend the night lying on the couch watching TV, but once you actually do it, you're usually happy you did.

Although the "have sex" solution to not having enough sex is, in my professional opinion, both effective and fun, a lot of people seem very worried about it. There is a Sub-Reddit for everything (the best beer to drink in the shower, for instance), and so perhaps it shouldn't surprise us that there is one for "Dead Bedrooms." It features a thread devoted to "sympathy sex." The thread provoked Kate Hakala, a writer for *Nerve*, to pen a polemic on why we should just stop having "sympathy sex" altogether. Her piece was impassioned, eloquent, and, I think, misguided.

Hakala says: "With the implication of pity sex comes the very troubling and incredibly dangerous implication that, sometimes, sex is owed to us." Why is this troubling and dangerous? Remember, we expect our partners to do something they may not want to do: Be faithful to us. Monogamy is a two-way street. Some people don't mind if their partner finds sex with someone besides us. But most of us do care. We think monogamy is owed to us.

I would propose a rule of thumb: You should care as much about making sure your partner is sexually satisfied as you care that he or she gets that satisfaction from you. It does not mean that you have to say "Yes" every time. It just means you should make a genuine, good-faith effort to meet your partner's needs as best you can. Now if you don't mind your partner going out and sleeping with someone else, fine. You're off the hook. But you should at least make that clear.

Hakala also claims that "treating sex as an errand raises a major gray area when it comes to questions of consent." I disagree – or at least I think that if there is a "major gray area" here, then we live much of our lives in that gray area. Imagine your partner says to you: "I sometimes find having dinner with your friends to be kind of an errand. Some nights I

do it not because I enjoy it but because I want to please you." Um, okay. So what? "Well," he says, "I think this raises a major gray area when it comes to con-sent. I'm not sure I'm really consenting to having dinner. Isn't it kind of like you're kidnapping me? And kidnapping is, you know, a crime." Your partner's mistake here is that he's failed to distinguish between being forced to do something against his will, and not getting to do exactly what he wants to do all the time. Having dinner with your partner's friends is kind of like being kidnapped. It's also kind of like being a mature adult who occasionally has to do things that aren't the exact things you most want to do at that exact moment.

Why might we think sex is different from going out for dinner? I can see two possibilities. One is that, at least for some people, sex is something inherently special. They think it should always be a magical act of soul-joining love. But I'm pretty sure Hakala doesn't think this, and I suspect most of my readers don't either. Another is linked to the troubling idea that men are somehow entitled to sexual access to women. This appallingly misogynistic idea has been promoted by so-called "pick up artists" and other self-pitying men, and it was for centuries embodied in law in the marital rape exception.

A woman was long presumed, on marriage, to grant her spouse free access to her body. Rape was defined as, in the words of Canada's 1892 criminal code, "the act of a man having carnal knowledge of a woman *who is not his wife* without her consent." (Emphasis added.) As this makes clear, so long as the

> *[Relationships are] work and negotiation – and negotiation about sex is always going to be a big part of that.*

couple were married, consent was not required. Feminist legal reformers are right to be proud of having gotten rid of this heinous idea, and you can't blame anyone for wanting to make sure we don't go back. And we must fight with all our energy the idea that sex is something women should provide men as a gender entitlement.

But we are talking here about something different: the role sex plays in building a relationship, and in contributing to the happiness of the partners within that relationship. And I doubt even the craziest war-on-women conservative would be willing to stand up and say: "You know, I was listening to Debby Herbenick talk about how we should all be game for what our partners want in the bedroom, and I found it very convincing. So maybe it's time to put the marriage exception back into rape law!"

There is one final argument that Hakala raises that I think deserves consideration. She asks: "If there is such a discrepancy in desire, why are you in the relationship?" But you could say this about any difference in preferences. Your partner likes the TV show *Supernatural* and wants you to watch it with her every Tuesday night. End the relationship! Your partner loves sushi. You're not crazy about it, but he wants you to take him to a Japanese restaurant every week or two. End the relationship!

Ideally, both partners should want sex at the same time. But ideally, both partners should, I guess, also like the same movies, want to hang out with the same people, and end up simultaneously eating the same piece of spaghetti from opposite ends of the plate, leading to constant, adorable, mid-noodle

smooches. If that happens, great. But, if it doesn't, we need to be prepared to cope.

We need to stop kidding ourselves that relationships are anything like we see in romantic comedies. They're work and negotiation – and negotiating about sex is always going to be a big part of that.

When the *Wall Street Journal* published a profile of a couple suffering from desire discrepancy, which emphasized the psychological costs to the low-desire partner (the husband), there was a flurry of reaction, much of it strongly negative.

The couple profiled by the *WSJ* were both conservative Mormons, who married as virgins and may not have been highly skilled at expressing their needs and desires. And the woman's low libido was clearly connected to the trauma of a miscarriage she had suffered early in the marriage. Commentators such as Amanda Hess were certainly right to point out that partners need to work to understand each other, and that desire discrepancy is a complex problem that requires sensitivity on both sides.

There are often deep issues – personal, relational and historical – that need to be worked through before a couple can connect with one another, and no amount of sex is going to do that on its own.

I am certainly not suggesting that couples ignore those issues, or that they avoid honest discussion about what they both want. My point is that, when you enter into a monogamous relationship with someone, they are, by definition, placing their sexual happiness in your hands. That's a trust we should all treat with the respect it deserves.

Sexual Honesty:
A Challenging and Empowering Journey

by Galen Fous

Finding a path to authentic expression of your most taboo sexual desire, from a place where it had been kept secret, is an empowering and healing journey.

I had a new client recently who confessed how she had almost turned around on her way to her first appointment. We had talked initially by email and then had a phone interview. She had asked for help in sorting out her secret sexual desires.

On the phone, she could only hint at what she had held back sexually all her life. In a choked voice, she struggled to say that it had to do with "being taken." She wanted to be dominated. "This is so embarrassing to talk about." Some part of her was terrified that she had this desire at all. It totally went against her feminist and religious beliefs. But she was reaching a point where her erotic desire was overwhelming her fear and shame at revealing it. She knew something had to shift. We scheduled an initial appointment for a talk-only session.

On the way, she had pulled over and parked down the street. She was in a battle with every part of her that wanted her to turn around and run away. She felt like she might throw up. Her body and soul were shaking in fear, just at the thought of telling the truth about the nature of her sexual desire. She had never revealed it to anyone before. She was nearly 50 years old.

But she also knew she was at the point of no return. It was clear to her, after all these years, her desire was not going away. Eros is such a relentless part of our being!

When she told me of her struggle just to arrive, I blessed her for her courage to confront and face the deep shame and fear she felt around her sexuality. Her story about the powerful urge to flee instead of show up drove it home for me once again:

It requires tremendous courage to overcome the deeply embedded fear and shame many of us carry around about our sexual truth. I am struck by the high percentage of my clients who have told me similar stories about their struggle not to turn around on the way to their appointment.

How is it that such an integral, natural, and vital part of who we are has become so vilified and repressed that we are compelled to hide it so desperately, and be so terrified of others knowing what our sexuality really looks like? Can it be anything but harmful to our physical, emotional, and spiritual well-being to live in a culture where we are afraid to speak the truth about our sexuality? Our culture provides no place where people can go to feel safe, honored, and encouraged to speak honestly about their erotic desires, at least those desires beyond the narrow range deemed appropriate by the conservative, sexually uptight mainstream.

It wasn't my intention to focus my practice on those who have never found a safe place, or someone they felt safe enough with, to reveal their most closely guarded sexual secrets. But somehow that has wound up being a good portion of my clients — those who reveal to me, for the first time ever, whatever sexual secrets they have held so guardedly, often for decades.

That is why I bless them for their amazing courage, just to show up! I am witnessing this Herculean effort by men and women who, despite their paralyzing fear, their overwhelming sense of guilt and shame, their bodies literally plunging into a state of flight, can still show up!

In this regard I am also struck by how deep, tenacious, and relentless the soul of Eros is. Despite decades of intense repression, fear, shame, and vilification, Eros does not go away. My clients tell stories of how they have tried to forget about what they desire sexually, channeled it into eating, drinking, irritability, frigidity, spirituality, or pornography. It did not matter! Eros was as strong a part of them as ever.

Many had tried to keep their Eros locked in a secret world of fantasy and masturbation. They were all deathly afraid of getting caught, but still took huge risks in some cases to feed their desire in shadowy, unconscious, or even dangerous ways.

I know exactly how my clients feel about revealing their sexual secrets. I came from the same place about 15 years ago. I had kept my interests in 'Fetish' and 'Kink' secret for my first 48 years, after a lifelong interest that be-

It requires tremendous courage to overcome the deeply embedded fear and shame many of us carry around about our sexual truth.

gan before puberty. I desperately hid it. I was so afraid of being judged, shamed, or punished socially. My outer persona, or my perfect cover, was the altar boy, the Eagle Scout, the gentleman, the guy in the white hat. The leap to becoming sexually authentic was terrifying. I could not imagine any way I could have the courage to take the leap. An unexpected nudge pushed me off the edge. It was a rough and tumble journey, but the blessings that came from being true to myself have forever enriched my life.

I am so grateful to be in a position now where I can offer the safety and trust that allows people to open up and speak their desire honestly. They can finally begin the process of learning about and sorting through the difficulties tangled up with their erotic desire. Healing is a process of disengaging the fear, shame, harsh judgments, feelings of not being worthy, and other challenges that have gotten embedded in the unconscious and that arise on cue, right along with our Eros.

This tangled up expression leaves us frozen, or clumsy, or disconnected physically, emotionally, and spiritually from the depth, power, and exhilaration that is natural to our sexual expression. This is why the path to sexual authenticity is quite often a powerful healing journey as well.

Sacred Sexuality and Sex

by Michael Picucci

To define sacred sexuality, it is important to rediscover what sex means to us. Paramount for growth in this area is to break out of preconceived thinking. To help us step out of the cultural box, I use the word "sex" as an acronym, S.E.X., which stands for Soul Energy eXchange, or as my partner sometimes likes to refer to it: Soul Energy eXtravaganza! Couple that with S.O.U.L., a Systemic Organization of Universal Love, as defined in the book, *The Living Energy Universe*, by Gary Schwartz and Linda Russek, and you have Soulful Sex.

This new perspective is not strictly about performance or procreation, or even about orgasm, though that can be a wonderful benefit. S.E.X. is about sharing and exchanging energies that originate more from our souls than just our heads or our genitals. It is about uniting our longing for wholeness and connection, yearnings that are naturally sacred and spiritual. It is about pleasuring and being pleasured in whatever consensual form that takes.

Author Brandy Williams writes:

"Sex is the most engrossing human act. Intimate touch involves all the senses. At the moment of pleasure, of shivering contact with a partner or a stolen moment of self-love, all our normal duties, tasks, fears, failures, all things we do drop away. This is life at its simplest, a time simply to be – to watch, listen, smell, taste, touch and feel, to focus on being a physical creature and experience the body's capacity for pleasure. [Indent omitted] When our bodies feel healthy and our hearts clear, when we can give and accept pleasure freely and with

sincerity, when we bring to intimate touch an awareness of the Divine, sex becomes sacred. We blossom into a fully human consciousness, caught up in the passionate embrace of life...We become...supple, flexible, centered, alive in the moment."

Sacred Sexuality

Sacred Sexuality is the desire to discover and explore both our conditioning and our limitations in exchanging four personal and distinct energies with another, or exploring them alone. We open our "new eyes and ears" and listen to our bodies through the felt senses. Becoming familiar with the body's felt senses adds great fluidity to the process. And, by expanding our sharing skills, however gradual, the experience of sacredness seeps into the bones and marrow of the lover.

What more beautiful way could human beings embody the sacred than by challenging themselves to bring the four primary soulful energies (see below) together? When we do this, when we consciously give and receive these four energies, we experience ecstasy, transcendence, and a new sphere of personal growth, empowerment, and understanding.

The Four Primary Energies

There are four primary soulful energies in Soul Energy Exchange (S.E.X.): love, pleasure, lingum, and yoni. The third and fourth energies are Hindu Sanskrit terms used by Tantra workshop leaders: Charles and Caroline Muir. Understanding them assists us in breaking out of our traditional, cultural thinking patterns.

The third expression, lingum energy, represents the masculine drive, penis, aggression and personal power, the giving of complex energies, and glory. While lingum energy is often male identified, in reality this energy is found in all human beings.

Our fourth soulful expression is yoni energy, which represents the feminine, the vagina or any part of the body that exudes surrender and desire to receive energy. Yes, men too have yoni energy.

We are all more or less conditioned and limited in our expression of yoni or lingum energies, not to mention love and pleasure. In truth we have all suffered traumas to our lingum and yoni energies, as well as love and pleasure. Unlocking traumatic and toxic shame, and thawing frozen energies are steps on our path to the sacred.

Experimenting, without judgment, along the felt sense boundaries of these energies is a direct route to god energy, the earth, our ancient memories, and the universe. All four of these soulful energies are the creator's way of expressing itself through us.

As the river gives into the ocean, what is inside me moves inside you…
– Robert Bly

Sexual Concerns

I have met with many people who have shared very personal sexual concerns with me. They ranged from feelings of deadness in their pelvis, to erectile challenges, orgasmic difficulties, being restricted in experiencing sexual desire, or feeling limited with a partner they love. Sometimes it's a body part, or image, thing – too big, too small, too tight, too wide. There are many similar burdens that people carry in a very heavy way. My experience

has taught me that the principles explored in my writing can be enormously helpful. In most of my experiences with *Focalizing*, a method I employ, these types of hardships have been resolved.

Integrating Spirituality & Sexuality

After facilitating countless workshops and sessions with individuals and couples, one thing is certain: The healing of the schism between our sexual and spiritual energies is not only a provocative topic, but one of the most intimidating tasks before us. Yet it is also one of the most important. What I call the "split" arises out of early religious and cultural training, which teaches that love and families are good, while sex is dirty, bad, and perverse. I have yet to meet one person who does not highlight this as a foremost challenge in life.

A deeply ingrained and culturally-induced rift between sexuality and spirituality haunts us. Yet, these two human forces are two sides of the same coin. At its most fundamental, when two people come together with open hearts, sex is a sacred act, joining them in body and spirit. This kind of union can be healing, the very embodiment of "transcendent beauty," to be regarded with reverence and respect.

All too often, this is clearly not the case. Opening the heart and keeping it open can be challenging particularly for those whose sexuality is connected to psychic and spiritual wounds of early experiences. As a result, it is difficult to resolve our connection to a "higher" power with our human need to express, satisfy, and celebrate our sexuality.

Healing the "Sexual-Spiritual Split"

The split between spirituality and sexuality is a deep psychic schism within almost everyone in our culture which prohibits enduring, loving relationships to form and continue to remain sexually alive and growing. This rift is caused by generational, cultural, religious, and early programming that plants seeds deep in the unconscious, which makes merging the two virtually impossible without specific healing.

The British author Aldous Huxley wrote, "The aim and purpose of life is the unitive knowledge of God." This speaks directly to the spiritual dilemma of our time: how to unite the polarities of our dissociative culture. Ever since Descartes said, "I think, therefore I am," we have been separating the body, mind, and spirit. I'm convinced that the key to the disconnecting dilemma we face is to reunite the body, mind, and spirit.

And a primary obstacle most people face is uniting the spiritual with the sexual. I call this "healing the sexual-spiritual split." We need to reintegrate God and the cosmos with our sexuality.

Relationships without Sacred Sexuality

When sex is not fulfilling in a monogamous relationship, the cornerstone of the union is weak and vulnerable. Most of us, consciously or unconsciously, commit to such relationships, at least in part, anticipating sexual satisfaction. If fulfillment dwindles or beco-

mes barely existent, a foundation of the relationship is betrayed. One will often feel imprisoned and act out in emotional or sexual ways. There is, or will soon be, "trouble in paradise." And often, because couples lack the skill required for sensitive dialogue, they go into denial, often for years. This is not necessary – new skills are available now.

I am happy to report that I have been living in a sexually fulfilling, loving relationship for many years now. All the work has been worth it! Opening up the heart, letting go of taboos, sharing shame-free sex, and being responsible and self-respecting, are keys to both the kingdoms of higher consciousness and pleasure. It

The healing of the schism between our sexual and spiritual energies is not only a provocative topic, but one of the most intimidating tasks before us.

is no wonder that when some are in the throes of orgasm they say, "Oh God, Yes!" In that moment of letting go and dropping defenses, a greater reality bursts forth. Loving sex heightens consciousness, and for me, God is consciousness, and pure consciousness is love.

Imagine yourself and your partner, with open hearts, choosing to pleasure each other. Imagine breathing and letting go into the bliss, whatever it may be, and knowing that you are going to God or the highest energy powers. Your partner is joining and supporting you in this awareness and experience. Then you switch, pleasuring your partner in whatever ways are desired and appropriate for the two of you.

If you really give yourself such a delightful experience, you will experience ecstatic sex, erotic energy, and you will have a rich spiritual experience that is enlightening as well. Each time another veil is lifted between partners, more consciousness opens up for them.

It will reveal itself in the daily living of life and in creative expression. This is what sex and pleasuring looks like when you are healing the sexual-spiritual split.

Sexuality & Higher Consciousness

Combining love with sexual expression can be an act of higher consciousness. In workshops, I help foster a genuine belief that when two human beings combine love's energy with erotic energies, a transcendent experience occurs, one that is often profoundly healing. This is a very sacred sharing and the true goal of a fulfilling sexual experience.

Reaching this goal is the result of a give and take, a negotiation of the open-hearted experience of interconnectedness.

Though this process can be awkward, it is essential to learn to communicate about our needs, desires, and fantasies. "Reclaiming Adolescent Awkwardness" is a phrase I use to give people permission to go to the awkward "places" necessary to heal the sexual-spiritual split and to form authentically intimate relationships.

Yet even so, we will often encounter resistance to fusing our loving, sexual and spiritual energies. Contrary to what many naively believe, we need to learn that healthy loving includes the expression of our more shadowy desires as well as our tenderness. The delicate opening up of our repressed sexual histories, variations, and fantasies is extraordinarily enriching and healing. Appreciating the nature of resistance and de-shaming our fantasies are

Opening up the heart, letting go of taboos, sharing shame-free sex, and being responsible and self-respecting, are keys to both the kingdoms of higher consciousness and pleasure.

entryways to a "circle of energy" allowing the experience of full body orgasm and full-hearted spirituality.

Under our needs, desires, and fantasies are powerful and subtle feelings and energies that want to be expressed. These expressions help us grow holistically; they teach us about aggression and passivity, about our feminine and masculine energies, and about pleasuring and being pleasured. They help us dissolve shame toward our inner contradictions and complexities and experience them fully for healing, growth, and self-understanding.

True and spiritual lovemaking is the interweaving choreography of our higher and shadow selves. It is a holistic fusing together of aspects of the so-called 'higher' and 'lower' self — how beautiful and so very intimate to do so with open hearts.

Evaluating Our Progress

I believe that there will always be one more way we can heal this schism, drop more veils, or enhance our capacity for pleasure and spirit. Not to worry. If all the veils were gone, where would our humanness be? How interesting to ponder such ideas as we heal ourselves day by day, and with each healing, enhance our ability to give and receive pleasure. It is a process of both struggle and delight with spontaneous expressions of perfection and bliss. Progress rather than perfection is the goal, and if we are earnest our bodies will lead our progress toward our personal perfection.

In evaluating our progress in healing our sexual-spiritual split, we need to ask ourselves: What motives do I bring to sexuality? What do I want from the sexual aspect of my nature? We know our healing is progressing when our answers emphasize spiritual fulfillment, integrating power and surrender, femininity and masculinity, and the desire for shared experiences of pleasure and higher consciousness.

Cracking the Code of Sexual Chemistry

by Stanley Siegel

We've all had the experience of seeing someone on the street or in a social setting and feeling an instant attraction. Our eyes lock, our pulse races, everyone else in the room disappears. Other times, attraction sneaks up on us slowly as we get to know someone. One day we realize that we are very sexually attracted to them. Whether it is their hair, body, voice, smell, or their attitude and behavior that attracts us, we attribute it to the mysteries of chemistry.

But chemistry isn't so mysterious. And, in my opinion, it's not what evolutionary scientists say: our instinctive way of knowing a prospective mate's reproductive potential and whether they possess the right set of genes.

On the contrary, chemistry begins in our thoughts. The subconscious mind reads signals and symbols – usually the physical traits and mannerisms of another person – and interprets them in relation to our individual fantasies. The body inspires our imagination – our reading of it echoes deeper psychological themes. We create a story grounded in our history. This happens so instantaneously that the details remain out of our awareness.

When there is a match between our fantasy and what a physical trait psychologically represents to us, we feel the excitement in our body.

A person whom we consider our sexual "type" possesses those qualities that we find highly attractive, though we often can't explain why. When the right signals appear, our fantasies will be ignited even though they may occur so instantaneously that we are not fully conscious of them. The ability to decode our attractions based on our sexual fantasies is essential to having smarter sex.

With practice, we can improve our ability to tune into sexual cues, what they mean and whether they are compatible with our true sexual desires. Armed with this knowledge, we increase our chances of choosing a partner with whom we are truly sexually compatible, as well as our potential to form a restorative experience that will be far more meaningful and satisfying than any sexual hook-up.

Marrying For Sex:
How to Find Sexual Compatibility
by Stanley Siegel

Just as we take into account such variables as personality, religion, family background, and education in choosing a prospective mate, sexual compatibility should be high on the list of considerations. Ideally, the process of self-discovery that takes place by following the steps of *Intelligent Lust* should happen before we choose a partner with whom we make a long-term commitment.

Too often we deny, suppress, police, or keep our erotic lives secret. In the process we disown an important part of who we are and may, as a result, choose the wrong partner. But if we set out to consciously identify our true sexual desires and the unmet need(s) from which they originate, they will tell us what is needed and who is best for us now. We can specifically choose a partner with whom we are deeply sexually and otherwise compatible, and who has the qualities that can enable us to further heal from those unresolved feelings for which our fantasies may act as antidotes.

After our initial attraction draws us to someone, we usually engage in a flirtation or acquaintanceship that can last a minute or for hours. During this engagement, we are more or less "turned on" depending on more subtle observations. When we follow the steps of *Intelligent Lust* (see "What Brings you to Orgasm?", we become conscious of whether a potential partner actually measures up to our fantasies and should be considered a prospect for moving forward. Though romance can certainly be an aspect of this, our pursuit is generally more substantial.

Of course, understanding our own sexual attractions and their psychological significance is only half of the sexual equation; discerning a potential partner's is the other.

Feeling strongly attracted to someone does not necessarily mean that his or her wants in bed will satisfy our deepest needs and desires. Whether we are already in a relationship or beginning one, what we learn from this step about the way we fit with a partner will determine the direction of the relationship. What we do next depends on what we discover about the similarities and differences in our desires.

Why? Because an essential element of sexual compatibility is the capacity to create a healthy restorative experience. And this requires openness, honesty, trust, and respect. Whether it's in the context of a brief encounter or ongoing relationship, we give preference to self-awareness, exploration, and authenticity over sexual performance or reaching an orgasm.

*   *   *

In a restorative experience, we create a safe and consensual encounter in which we act out with our partner a fantasy we have privately imagined, whose symbolic meaning we have already come to understand.

Whether the scenario is as conventional as romantic seduction, or as unusual as extreme bondage fantasies, we connect – physically, emotionally, and spiritually with the deepest part of our psyches, recovering what was previously suppressed or denied. In the process, we restore ourselves to wholeness. A restorative experience can have a profound emotional and spiritual effect on us.

Of course, the deepest and most lasting healing comes when we have the opportunity to experience our true desires and work through the mastery of the conflicts behind them over time. Whether it's with a lover or spouse, a restorative relationship assumes an emotional posture that is often diametrically opposite from the dysfunctional ones we experienced in our childhood.

Why?
Because an essential element of sexual compatibility is the capacity to create a healthy restorative experience.

Characterized by openness, intimacy, and mutual respect, the new relationship allows us to derive a new settlement to old conflicts or needs. Within this friendship, sex is not separated from the joys and struggles of daily life, nor diminished by its challenges. Instead, it offers a rich and fertile ground for a meaningful and satisfying life.

If we've come this far in following the steps of *Intelligent Lust*, we've learned that it's not just good sex we're after, but also an experience that takes us to a level far from the mundane into the realm of the ecstatic.

*   *   *

How do we find out if we are sexually compatible with a potential partner without first having sex?

The answer is one that cannot be found in the typical dating guide. We can take a proactive approach, gradually engaging a partner in open, honest, and frank conversations about their sexual experiences and desires. Res-

pect, understanding, affection, and friendship are inseparable when two people enter into conversation fully present. Its radiance branches out. Directly talking about sex not only helps us discern someone's sexual preferences and whether they match our own, but also gives us a strong indication of the level of intimacy that we can achieve with someone.

Talking about sex with someone we've recently met may feel embarrassing or uncomfortable at first, because it requires breaking social or familial conventions, perhaps challenging our current taste and values. But such direct communication is the best way to help clarify the similarities and differences in attitudes and desires. If we are already in a long-term relationship, we can gain greater insight into the truth about the sexual difficulties we are experiencing with a partner. If we are to become truly sexual, we need to be vulnerable and open, even willing to be shocked by the nature of a partner's response.

Typically, because of social training, women find intimate conversation easier, while men tend to be squeamish and avoid such matters, though men or women who have suffered sexual abuse may be reluctant to talk about sex at all. Gay men, on the other hand, seem to find talking about sex much easier. Since, from an early age, they have been forced to navigate issues of sexuality in a hostile world, ideas about sex are in the forefront of their consciousness. It's not unusual, during a first encounter, for a gay man to ask a potential sexual partner, "What are you into?"

But for most of us, such conversation usually arouses strong emotional reactions. Some of us may feel ashamed, while others find talking about sex unromantic. Some of us are not great communicators, while others may be naive and find the idea of sexual compatibility too complex to consider. Some think that talking about sex takes its spontaneity away, that sex will lose its allure. And still others just want to "get laid." A man who brings up sex early in dating might be considered creepy, if not a predator. Even couples in long-term relationships often have an unspoken agreement not to talk about sex.

When we do talk about sex, we learn more than simply the content of someone's sexual inclinations. How the person talks about sex gives us important information. Perhaps they are too shy or skittish or unusually over-confident. Maybe they blatantly refuse to discuss sex. No matter how strong the chemistry, these can be signs of incompatibility.

Introducing conversation about sex requires sensitivity. It's important to choose the right time and circumstances, which should include privacy, an environment with no ditractions, the opportunity for eye contact, and enough time for a conversation not to be rushed. It also demands a supportive, non-judgmental attitude. We need to open our hearts and imaginations and be willing to listen, regardless of what comes up. We suspend the usual rules of etiquette and enter as deeply as possible into the passion and imagination of someone else.

Some say the excitement of blindly discovering a partner's sexuality is half the plea-

> *Respect, understanding, affection, and friendship are inseparable when two people enter into conversation fully present.*

sure, but it just as often leads to misunderstand and failure. What we might lose in spontaneity, we gain in understanding and purpose.

Sexually Speaking

Use these questions to help frame a conversation with a potential partner. If you are already in a well-established relationship, the intimacy necessary in completing this step – whatever the outcome – is likely to be beyond anything you've ever experienced before.

For now, scan these questions to see how much you know about how your partner would respond.

For those of you who have found someone you're interested in, choose the questions that are most relevant to you and put them in your own words. While some conversations develop naturally after watching a romantic movie or TV show, it's just as likely you'll need to orchestrate one. How a potential partner handles these conversations is as important as their answers.

- What's the best sexual experience you've had with a partner?
- What was the worst?
- Are most of your sexual experiences satisfying?
- What do you find missing in your sexual experience with most partners?
- Is there anything you've asked a partner to do during sex that he or she refused to do?
- What's your ideal sexual experience?
- Are there sexual experiences you've fantasized about, but never had?

- What do you fear most in a sexual experience?
- Is there a lot of variety in your sexual behavior or do you prefer doing one particular thing?
- Do you believe it's more important to focus on getting yourself or your partner off, or focus on the experience of sex?
- How often do you like having sex? Do you prefer one time of day over another?
- What do you do when you want to have sex and your partner doesn't?
- How important do you think sex is in a relationship?
- How sexually experienced do you think you are?
- How do you communicate what you want sexually? Is it more through actions or words?
- How open are you to new adventures?
- Do you like to take your time or prefer brief sex?
- Have your former partners complained or said anything negative about your sexual behavior?
- Are there places you prefer not to be touched?
- What do you like to do after having sex? Do you prefer to hang out in bed or get on with life?

After these conversations you will have a good understanding of where your partner is with their sexuality and also, if you've followed the previous steps of *Intelligent Lust*, a context for making sense of where their feelings come from and what they mean. You will understand the childhood conflicts that underlie them and what they are attempting to heal. It will also naturally deepen your compassion for your partner, whether or not you are sexually compatible.

What a Sex Therapist Does

by Alyssa Siegel

I found my way into sex therapy inadvertently. I didn't set out to specialize in it, but after working with individuals and couples for many years and finding the conversation inevitably turning to sex and sexuality, I came to understand that there is a desperate need for counselors who are willing to talk openly and frankly about their clients' most intimate thoughts, sexual practices, sexual fantasies.

Unfortunately many counselors feel uncomfortable or embarrassed and may change the subject, sometimes unconsciously, during a session when sex comes up. Growing up in a sex-positive household in which questions about sex were openly welcomed rather than shamed, talking about sex comes easily and naturally to me. Because I myself have thoroughly explored my own sexuality and sexual attitudes, rather than deflecting conversation, I am comfortable creating the space for others to discover their own.

Over the years, I familiarized myself with the writings of experts, attended lectures and professional trainings, joined associations and groups that supported openness and held sex-positive attitudes, and thoroughly investigated my own assumptions, even biases about sex, eventually qualifying myself as a sex therapist.

There are many misconceptions about what a sex therapist does. Other than an ethical agreement regarding no physical contact, sex therapists practice using different approaches, from simple sex education to making suggestions about how to spice up a client's sex life.

Much of my work involves helping people understand their sexual desires, honor them, and create opportunities to express them. We spend a good deal of time exploring sexual beliefs, fantasies, past experience, sexual identity, and gender issues within the wider context of the client's psycho-sexual history. Not surprisingly, the largest group of clients who seeks sex therapy are trauma survivors. The sad reality is that many people with sexual conflicts have experienced some form of sexual abuse or assault in their lives, which impacts their current sex life.

Our relationship with sex is far more complex than we assume. Most of us struggle with it at some point in our lives. And it's especially difficult maintaining a satisfying and meaningful sex life with a partner with whom we are sharing our life.

Why? To start, many people simply have not invested a lot of time in exploring their sexuality. Men seem at a disadvantage here, because the first exposure most boys have to sex is often pornography; in the past, it may have been through the glossy naked photos of women in dad's *Playboy*, and now it's internet pornography with overwhelming displays of men with large and ever-ready penises, and women willing to do whatever it takes to satisfy a man's need to get off.

These images are misogynistic and cartoonish in their illustrations of what sex is and who is sexy. Girls, on the other hand, are more likely to discuss sex with peers and work a little harder to figure out their bodies and what feels good, because it is less straight forward than for boys. But, where women may have a slight socialization advantage, we are at a severe disadvantage when it comes to being taught that our needs and wants actually matter.

Consequently, we grow ashamed, blame ourselves for having desires and fantasies, and eventually pathologize them.

A psychological defense such as detachment or dissociation that served to protect against overwhelming emotions in the past, gets triggered automatically in sexual situations in the present.

author – Stanley Siegel, my father, suggests that most individuals are skipping the fundamental processes of learning about their true sexual selves and therefore do not have the ability to determine sexual compatibility with a partner before they make a long-term commitment.

Sex has a different meaning for everyone. For some, it is a way to create and foster intimacy. For others, sex can only happen after intimacy and trust have been established. Sometimes partners may not be on the same page. The difference in sexual approaches may lead to conflict that may be difficult to resolve and painful to discuss.

For most of us, sexual interest tends to ebb and flow based on many factors — psychological, biological, emotional, and circumstantial. It's not unusual for those in long-term relationships to experience different levels of sexual interest over the life of the relationship.

In *Sexual Intelligence*, Marty Klein suggests that we rely too much on the assumption that sex should be easy (our youthful hormones and the immaturity of our relationships inform this belief) and that we don't need to make the adaptive changes necessary as we age or spend longer periods of time with a partner to keep sex satisfying.

In *Mating in Captivity* by Esther Perel, the author writes that intimacy kills desire because it is hard to marry desire with the familiarity that occurs between partners whose life is so coalesced with your own.

In *Your Brain on Sex: How Smarter Sex Can Change Your Life* – of which I am a contributing

To complicate matters, during sex, most of us are as much engaged in our private thoughts and fantasies as we are in what is actually occurring. We may be thinking about what our partner thinks about us; how we smell, feel, or taste; whether we are a good lover; if we're disappointed with their body; how we measure up to their other partners? And sometimes we may fantasize about a sexual act other than what we are involved with or even sex with a different partner.

It's a wonder any of us ever has sex. And some of us don't.

Clients who seek therapy with me generally fall into three categories: (1) those who are struggling because they have reached a sexual impasse with their partner (sex has slowed or stopped completely and one or both partners are concerned or unhappy about it); (2) clients who feel they have some sort of sexual "dysfunction" such as premature ejaculation, inability to get or maintain an erection, a "low" libido, or an inability to orgasm; and (3) those whose lead lives in which their sexual practices or identity are considered somehow "fringe" or "non-traditional" — queer, poly-, or trans- clients, for example, practice kink or engage in a fetish or sexual behavior relating to their sexuality which has led to criticism and judgement. Because they have been forced to consider their differentness in relationship to sex, these clients are actually among the most sex savvy.

For some, therapy involves facilitating a safe dialogue around sex. Many have never talked openly and directly about their sexual desires. I focus conversation on what role sex plays in each partner's history and psychology — what each of their preferences are and how they come together and diverge in their interests. Unraveling a partner's sexual history can take time, especially if trust is not a natural part of the relationship or if it has been breached by an affair or other event.

Sometimes, both partners may be inexperienced with sex or have different levels of experience. Beyond conversation, they may require encouragement to experiment, as well as guidance or specific strategies geared towards acting out their desires.

The most common issue couples present is that sex has decreased or stopped in their relationship and this has caused an oppressive tension between them. The problem with less or no sex in a relationship for any given period of time is not that there is anything inherently wrong with it, but that people apply meaning and significance to what they believe the change must represent. From this they will often act out, coming from a place of fear or rejection. They might withdraw, retaliate, or seek out sexual desire and validation from others.

This kind of sexual impasse is both the best and the worst of sexual conflicts because in a lot of cases, sex was once good between partners and finding it again, with some open and compassionate conversation and ideas, is highly possible. But if this doesn't happen, the issue builds its own momentum and can poison a relationship, making it so toxic and damaging that partners ultimately part ways.

The ways in which I help couples return to sex are varied. For some it is simply a matter a facilitating a safe dialogue around it. For others it may look more like a discussion of specific strategies geared towards pleasurable touch. In both cases it is a process of discovery, of shedding light on the role sex plays in each partner's being and learning where preferences come together and diverge in a respectful way. It can take time, depending on where the couple is starting from and if they are trying to recover from something such as a wound in trust, but it can happen.

The coming back together is truly wonderful.

In some cases, partners are sexually incompatible and unable to navigate a sex life that works for both. While it can be a matter of differing sexual preferences, more often a satisfying sex life can't be achieved because the underlying issue is more about power and control than it is about sexual differences. Rather than functioning as a team in which both partners' feelings and desires are honored, one or both partners are caught up in thinking, "How can I get my partner to do it *my* way?"

I recently counseled a couple in which one partner wanted an open, or 'poly', relationship and the other believed strongly in monogamy. Frank conversations could not resolve the issue. Both decided their difference was intolerable; they made the decision to part.

In another case, one partner had a strong desire to act out BDSM fantasies (the safe and consensual Bondage, Domination, Sadistic and Masochistic acts of sexual play abusively misconstrued by popular media like "Fifty Shades of Grey"), while the other felt a strong distaste for bondage. Detailed conversations about sex, reading books, and watching videos provided an "education" about BDSM that helped the reluctant partner understand the structure, safety, and communication that went into such play.

Her education freed her to experiment, which over time she found both liberating and satisfying. The 'kinky' partner, on the other hand, was asked to make some compromises of his own about certain practices that would remain off-limits.

Typically when a client comes to me with a self-diagnosed sexual dysfunction, I first direct them to a medical doctor to rule out very real physical complications. When a difficulty cannot be explained medically, there may be an emotional trauma at its root.

Sexual trauma can impact survivors in a multitude of ways both internally (desires, fantasies) and externally (physical response cycles and sexual practices). Its effects can crop back up even when we believe we've "put it behind us." A psychological defense such as detachment or dissociation that served to protect against overwhelming emotions in the past, gets triggered automatically in sexual situations in the present. Before we know it, we have lost our erection, experience dryness or pain, or we have lost interest in sex altogether.

Survivors often have a long journey, and their partner's is challenging as well. I coach partners to be patient — to maintain a solid sense of self, to learn what their partner's triggers are but not to take their partner's triggered reactions personally when they are inadvertently happened upon. With the right attitude, it is a precious opportunity for growth. *Healing Sex: A Mind-Body Approach to Healing Sexual Trauma,* by Staci Haines does a beautiful job of describing this.

For those who have not experienced sexual trauma, I see a vicious cycle at the root of sexual dysfunction. One incident of premature ejaculation or a lost erection, for instance, creates such fear, anxiety, and self-doubt that we become consumed with the thought that our body will not cooperate, turning it into our enemy. As a result we might develop performance anxiety before sex or avoid it altogether.

There are a few "quick fix" solutions to delay ejaculation or prolong erections that I relay to clients that often break the cycle of failure, but the longest term benefit comes when we practice mindfulness; when we learn to be in the present moment by focusing on our breath. Typically, when we have conflict over sex we hold our breath. This sends a message to our brain to be on alert, a message in conflict with what is needed in order to let go and surrender to a sexual experience. By opening our breath, we can return to the present and allow the experience to flow without expectation.

For those clients with sexual interests or identities far outside the norm, therapy must have a strong element of support and acceptance because of the effects discrimination and oppression may have had on them. Many of these clients have already developed a strong sense of self-awareness as well as the courage necessary to forge their own path where there haven't been maps to follow. In forming a polyamorous or open relationship, therapy can now help them learn to better manage complicated personal dynamics, establish rules to navigate jealousy, rivalry, loyalty, and respect, and develop communication skills along with a high level of personal responsibility and accountability.

*   *   *

Think back, for a moment, to when you first learned about sex. Was it an awkward, brief, or cautionary conversation with your parents, the preachings of your church, a sex education class at school that warned about pregnancy and STD's, or the media? Few people have positive or open-minded introductions to the world of sex. With misinformmation, misassumptions, myths, and half-truths fill the gaps of all that we do not know.

Too many of us feel hurt, embarrassment, and shame because of misconceptions about what it means to be sexually healthy. When it comes to sex, there is no "normal." Sexual fantasies and practices are incredibly diverse and original despite what we are led to believe. So long as sex is consensual — asking a partner if they want to proceed, or as complex as specific arrangements made with multiple partners — sex can be meaningful and gratifying.

Our sexual desires have origins that stretch far back into our earliest experiences, before we even knew what sex was. Many of the clients I've worked with are afraid to share their fantasies and desires because they worry about what their partner may think of them. The common fantasy of dominating or of being dominated, for instance, may be in direct opposition to a desire for true equality in all other aspects of a relationship and therefore may never be discussed.

It's important to remember that when we deny, repress, or bury our sexual fantasies, we grow alienated from who we truly are. Knowing and honoring our desires is essential to our sense of well-being. We always have the choice to limit their expression to the bedroom or design a life style around them depending on the depth of our needs and the authenticity of the relationship we create with a partner.

Survivors often have a long journey, and their partner's is challenging as well.

I deeply believe in the power of sex therapy to repair misconceptions, heal sexual wounds, and open the doors to more meaningful, creative, and gratifying sex.

I feel grateful every day that this profession found me. I am honored to have the opportunity to join many like-minded others in creating a more accepting and positive view of sex so that our children may avoid the conflict and suffering inflicted by repressive ideologies, whether they originate in religious fundamentalism or even in the field of psychology.

Sex Worker or Therapist?

by Stanley Siegel

"Sex Worker or Therapist?" was censored by *Psychology Today* after its initial publication in 2012 and never appeared online

Several years ago, a 62-year-old man had a consultation with me a few months after good friends had conducted, let's say, an intervention on his behalf. Andrew was a pediatrician who had worked nearly his whole life in rural Vietnam, a demanding job that caused him to sideline other important parts of his life. Now that he had retired, his friends decided Andrew needed help building a sex life. He accepted their rather unconventional assistance.

Andrew told me he always knew he was gay even though until recently he had never had sex with anyone. "For the first time in my life," he said. "I've developed an intense excitement about having sex with men and perhaps even a loving relationship."

I asked him about the recent sexual experience arranged by his friends.

"They found an escort for me. It was a little like you see in the movies — the father taking his virgin son to see a prostitute to initiate him into manhood. Having done their research, my friends chose well. The young man understood that I was a virgin and was extraordinarily kind, loving, and generous with me. I was terrified and overexcited. He handled me perfectly," Andrew said.

"Since then, I've seen Peter weekly. It's been the most amazing experience. I am learning to appreciate my body as old as it is and I'm also learning the mechanics of sex which I had only occasionally seen in porn movies. My whole attitude has changed. I feel much more confident about myself and I've started

to date. I'm so grateful to Peter for what he is giving to me."

Another patient, Judith, reported that in the past she had seen a male escort who helped her with a deep fear. Judith had several disturbing childhood experiences with an uncle who fondled her, sometimes masturbating while he touched her pre-pubescent breast.

Judith had consequently developed a life-long fear of physical contact with men, and although she had fantasized regularly about having sex, when she expressed her fears to the men she dated, they inevitably left her. "Too much baggage," she said. "As it turned out the right man for me was an escort."

"I confided my fears in my closest girlfriend," she continued. "She made the suggestion that I try an escort. I thought she was nuts at first, but it was absolutely the right thing. I found an escort service online and called. Dan was sweet, tender, and gentle. He knew exactly how to touch me. He had a lot of patience that guys I dated didn't have. I saw him about four or five times and while I am not entirely cured, I am on the way. I'm no longer afraid the way I was. I'm making better choices with men now because of Dan."

Later, she said, "It didn't matter at all that I was paying him. I've paid more to therapists over the years and I didn't get anywhere." She added one more thought. "I got attached to him, maybe I even felt a kind of love. But, I got over it quickly. I put it in its place. Yet I have to say that it opened my heart to other men in a way I couldn't before." Like Andrew, time with a sex worker prepared Judith to go out into the world with experience, self-confidence, and a positive attitude toward sex. She felt she could finally have a sexual relationship.

Every escort might not have the same talents to heal, and while some do exploit their clients, the sex workers I spoke with, as well as some I have been with, share many of the same positive values and ethics as therapists. Both psychotherapists and sex workers have guided me, at different times in my life, to a deeper understanding of my true desires, partly by challenging me to confront shame.

Of course, a sex worker's profession is illegal in most states.

In the 1970s, sex researchers Masters and Johnson introduced the idea of using sexual surrogates with patients to engage in intimate sexual relations to achieve a therapeutic goal. The idea caught on for a short time. Sex surrogates were eventually certified to use a combination of techniques — talking, listening, and performing to help resolve a patient's sexual issue(s). Psychotherapists referred patients to sex surrogates who had problems with self-confidence, sexual anxiety, premature ejaculation, vaginismus, sexual inhibition, and erectile dysfunction.

Despite the high success rate of surrogate programs, complicated legal issues, along with intense criticism from both the far right and feminist organizations, arose. Few states allow sexual surrogates to practice these days.

The sex worker industry, on the other hand, will never disappear. And while therapists cannot refer patients to them, they are working with mental health professionals to help patients explore and develop their sexual potential.

Of course, communication plays a key role in the success of these sexual exchanges, as it does in therapy, since so many sexual issues are psychological. I have heard of sex workers who use relaxation techniques, intimate verbal communication, non-genital contact, sexual touching, as well as intercourse.

Because of negative attitudes associated with prostitution, we think of it as lacking humanity. After all, it's an activity engaged in mostly by strangers with an exchange of money. Therefore, we make the wrong assumption that both parties are entering into a very intimate encounter with total detachment.

But this wasn't the case with my patients, nor with some of the sex workers I interviewed.

"I've had such positive experiences with hookers," one straight patient told me. "The best experiences have been the conversations. Some are better educated than I am. They seem to genuinely enjoy their work and care about their clients. We are no different. We're all people. I'm sure their relationships are just as fraught with complications as mine. The only shame I have about it is what society places on me. I wouldn't talk about it with my friends, even though I've learned so much about sex and myself through these experiences. My guy friends would think that I'm not cool enough to find and keep a girlfriend and my female friends would be totally creeped out. I wish I could openly recommend it to my friends, but I can't.

I wanted to learn more about the views of escorts.

"I introduce guys to their bodies," one woman I met online told me. "Most of the men I meet are pretty out of touch with themselves physically. They think they want to just fuck. I teach them that sex isn't all about fucking. I relax them first with conversation, then sensual touching. I teach them what women need. The connection is important. "Sometimes I'll ask a client about his fantasies if I feel comfortable enough with him. They don't always know until I coax it out of them. If we're sexually compatible, then we will go ahead and try to play his fantasies out. There are times I'm just not into what a guy wants and will politely tell him that he would have a better experience with someone who enjoys what he does. I do it without shaming him.

"Don't get me wrong. I'm not entirely a missionary. I enjoy the money. There is something erotic about getting paid. It's as much a turn-on as anything else. It satisfies a deep need of mine to be admired."

I spoke with Devon Hunter, a gay man who has a decade of experience in the adult entertainment industry and who became a sex worker, or courtesan, as he prefers to call himself, after years of deliberation.

"What motivates me is the desire to create an experience that awakens kindness and compassion in my clients. Most of my clients are not coming to have intercourse. The great majority seek intimacy and affection. I create a boyfriend experience in which we get acquainted through conversation, touch, perhaps tender kissing. We might go out to dinner then come home and have sex, but just as often not. Together, we establish a romanticized, or idealized version of what every man hopes for. In part, I accomplish this by focusing my attention with deep compassion and empathy for what it is someone needs, whatever they look like, act like, or fantasize. I suspend all judgements. My goal is to affirm people.

"Some of these men come from relationships that are dysfunctional or codependent where there has been sacrifice. Our experience acts as a counterpoint. It's healing in that my client internalizes the kindness, compassion, and tenderness we exchange, then takes that into his own life and propagates it. Although I am not trained as a therapist, I always hope that the experience is a therapeutic one for my client. That doesn't mean that it's not sexy.

"I develop a bond with clients as regularly as might happen in real life, and it's as authentic as any that would happen outside of the situation. It grows from the cycle of freely giving and receiving that I work to establish. Being a man is demanding. Men have to prove they are men, usually through aggressive behavior.

"When we are together, we can suspend that performance. Often I teach a client to receive. To let me take care of them. Most realize that intercourse is not what they want. Affection and sensuality are what's most meaningful to them, often achieved simply through kissing.

"Unfortunately, sex workers are marginalized and demonized on all fronts. I understand there are people who are hustlers — 'gay for pay.' They are often men who are self-loathing, emotionally inauthentic, and inaccessible. Those kind of people exist in every profession. Some men are sadly attracted to the danger and potential self-destructiveness of encounters with these men.

"I want to bring attention to the fact that while sex workers have to constantly deal with society's demonization of them, many are not self-hating. Personally, such ostracism reminds me to act with greater kindness and empathy towards everyone."

It's difficult not to continue the comparison between the goals and techniques of these sex workers and of psychotherapists — empathy, compassion, communication and connection, self-knowledge, affirmation, and a corrective experience. Both experiences take place within a suspended reality where the relationship is limited to a prescribed time and place.

I remember sitting in the lobby of an office suite I once shared. Several patients sat on either side of me and I imagined what it would be like for them waiting for their session to start.

My watch read 12:50 p.m. Suddenly, the doors of a dozen consultation rooms flung open. It was the end of the patients' fifty-minute session. They were followed a minute later by nearly twelve therapists who came out for a stretch or bathroom break

The image of sex workers standing outside their doors, waiting for their next client in Amsterdam's bustling Red Light District, instantly came to mind.

The Cuddler

by Anonymous

In my mind's eye, I am backstage behind a curtain while Oprah tells her studio audience they are about to meet a man who paid a woman to cuddle with him. Her announcement is met with gasps, skeptical laughter, and facial expressions betraying attempts to wrap the mind around such a concept.

It's true: I paid Sam Hess, the professional cuddler in Portland, Oregon, to cuddle with me for an hour.

You'll have a hard time convincing me it was just a coincidence that less than 24 hours later, my doctor's office recorded my lowest blood-pressure reading in years. Or that post-cuddle I felt better physically and emotionally than I had in a long time.

Why did I pay $80 for 60 minutes of snuggling next to a stranger, in my queen-size bed? I could say I thought it would be an interesting topic to write about for you after I first read about her in the Oregonian newspaper. I could say that at a time when I had a heightened awareness of people carving out creative careers for themselves in this new economy, I was intellectually curious. Those reasons are true and valid, but I also wanted someone to hold me – and someone to hold. It had been a long time. I needed it.

I know you have questions: about her background, her motivation, how she sets boundaries, and so much more. The FAQ at CuddleUpToMe.com has your answers, and I recommend reading her site for context. What I hope to do in this space is to put you in the experience with her, as best I can.

A mandatory part of the process is a face-to-face meeting in a public place before a session is even scheduled. Sam and I met at a coffee shop, nearly three weeks after I first emailed her and asked for a session, and we talked for an hour. Yes, to prepare for an hour of snuggling with a new client, she spent an hour of her time with me and drove an hour round-trip for the meeting. There she was, 5 feet tall, not even 120 pounds, and there I was, towering over her inside a bustling Starbucks.

Let me tell you: She was in charge. She wanted to know about me, and she remarked that I was more guarded than most of her clients, and she had to gently nudge me a bit to get me to reveal enough for her to understand why I wanted to cuddle with her. The more time I spent with her, the more I found myself saying things I was surprised to hear myself saying to someone I'd just met. There is something about her that invites you to open up to her, even as your resistance remains high.

We scheduled the appointment for two weeks later. (That's 34 days from the initial email to the day of the cuddling, which gives you an idea of how far in advance she was booked.) The night before my session, I did laundry, chose the clothes I would wear, and made sure to allow time to shower, shave and brush my teeth before she arrived at my place.

When I awoke early on the morning of the session, I was instantly reminded of one of the questions in her FAQ: What about "natural reactions"? Yes, I woke up that morning with an erection, and I began to wonder if it would happen as we cuddled, and how we would react. I tried not to let it worry me, and her answer on the FAQ page helped: "This will happen from time to time. When these things come about we just change positions so that it does not become a focus of the session."

She arrived a few minutes late. We hugged at the door, and I realized I was meeting her full embrace with one of those patented 'guy hugs,' with plenty of nervous, no-idea-what-to-do-with-this-feeling pats on her back, which I'm sure was the first of many clues that I was several layers of emotional protection removed from her open, giving nature.

We talked for a few minutes about the weather, and then I paid her, to get that out of the way. I asked her how a session usually begins, and she told me to get in whatever position I wanted — on the couch, in bed, wherever — and she would come to me. She offered to play music from her iPhone if I wanted that, and I opted to begin with no music and perhaps ask for some later if I wanted. As it turned out, we never put on any music.

I got into my most relaxing position, to start: on my back, on the right side of my bed. All along I'd wondered if I could be comfortable spooning at first, and actually I just love having a woman rest her head on my shoulder. Without my having said so, she crawled into bed and got into that position, snuggled up against me on my left side, with her head on my left shoulder.

As she had at the coffee shop two weeks earlier, she could sense my holding back. One of her first comments to me during the cuddle session was about my noticeable nervousness. Well, with me it's a dead giveaway. I don't have the steadiest hands, and my body feels like it's in a perpetual state of anxiety, with an

My reasons were honorable, but in so doing I came off as keeping a bit of distance, and truth be told, no doubt I was protecting myself as well.

elevated heartbeat and borderline high blood pressure. But it was an amazing sensation in those first few minutes feeling someone nestled in that spot on my left side, near my heart, and things changed. She touched my face, and I touched her hair. Skin touched skin in different places, all of them appropriate relative to her boundaries, and we began to hold more tightly to each other.

In the weeks leading up to the session, I'd had so many worries. What if I get sweaty? What if my stomach growls? What if my body does any number of things it seems to do more frequently and awkwardly the older I get? What if I have a cramp or a spasm? Or if I sneeze? Oh, why am I doing this?

She and I talked about this next aspect moments after I became aware of it, but it was a revelation to me how muscle memory came into play. Yes, it had been a long time since I had cuddled with someone, but my hands and body began to touch and stroke naturally, like a reflex. It was as if the part of me that knew how to tenderly touch a woman had been frozen by cryogenics, in a state of suspended animation, and upon awaking, it knew instinctively what to do.

Of course, there is an aspect to this I think probably speaks to some of the differences between men and women and their experience of cuddling – that it's easy for that muscle memory to lead to a level of touching beyond the mere cuddle. In my experience (and I think I'm not alone), women have a much easier time separating cuddling touch from other forms of touch.

That's not as easy for men to compartmentalize. I had to monitor myself, check myself, to ensure I was not in any danger of touching her inappropriately. If I had allowed my body to completely take over and not involved my mind, who's to say? When I addressed this with her moments after realizing it, she told me, "Don't worry; I am in control," reassuring me that she knew how to protect her boundaries. It was then that I became aware of the strength in her tiny body. The grip of her legs around mine may well have been a natural part of her cuddling, but it served her well in letting me feel her power, which could easily be dismissed by simply looking at her.

After an hour of snuggling with her, I believe the same energy that flows from her and heals also invests the kind of strength that allows her to feel in control, and in fact to be in control.

In terms of touch, I probably erred on the side of caution, which I'm sure made me seem even more like I was holding back. My reasons were honorable, but in so doing I came off as keeping a bit of distance, and truth be told, no doubt I was protecting myself as well.

Prolonged eye contact up close was difficult for me at first, and she noticed. I think there has to be a certain allowance for the fact that you're in bed with someone with whom you've spent little more than an hour, someone you'd never met before that coffee shop meet-and-greet.

Sam has such active eyes; even when they are still and focused, they are communicating so much, and I felt them saying what she'd told me was the goal of a session: to let someone feel unconditional love and acceptance, and to feel human touch and its many benefits. There is so much empathy in her eyes, and it can easily draw out emotion — and the same is true of her touch.

"This is hard for you," she said, alluding to how I could go only so long with direct eye contact before pulling her close to me in a tighter bear hug. I needed the embrace, yes, but I'm willing to concede that I needed to retreat from the intimacy of extended eye-contact. Know this: I consider none of that a reflection of her, or her eyes; rather, it's all about me and my insecurities, and needing my bubble.

But wow, I'd forgotten what it was like to touch a woman, stroke her hair, feel her face, put my fingertips on the back of her neck. I had often found myself wondering if I even remembered how to touch someone in a way that made them feel good. The part of me that has wanted for so long to be intimate and sexually active again, which has been building with intensity lately, was naturally curious as I touched Sam. Does this feel good? And a two-pronged question: Is this arousing in any way? If yes, great; I still know how to touch another person and stoke her fire. But then, the realization: That's not what this is about. Be careful. Don't let yourself go down that slippery slope.

Still, I couldn't help but think that cuddling with Sam was an important part of preparing for relationship intimacy again, peeling off my layers a bit at a time, allowing someone to hold me and not my armor when I am finally in someone's arms again, and she in mine. There is probably some value in the flip side, in allowing that person to be the one to do the peeling, but I sensed my cuddling time with Sam was a precursor to creating a comfort level with human contact I would not have otherwise been able to nurture. Although it might have nothing to do with Sam's purpose, it felt like a wonderful byproduct of the experience, of her therapy.

I use that word intentionally: therapy. I'll leave it for you to evaluate her credentials, but I consider Sam a therapist, someone skilled in the healing arts, and after reading her website and spending two hours with her, I know this is a person with a plan, a purpose, a methodology, a gift, and a wonderful way of pulling together her innate qualities and learned techniques to develop a powerful dynamic. At one point I said to her, "You know what you're doing." She said, "Yes, I do." She is following a plan, but it clearly comes from her heart. You can't look into her eyes and come to any other conclusion.

At the very least, her cuddle sessions are a wonderful exercise in aspects of nonsexual touching. She said she's a nonverbal communicator, and that's so true. I asked her where her empathy comes from, as the analytical side of me is curious, and has been, and she told me a personal story detailing its history.

Hers is a story for her to tell at her choosing, and not for me to share. But, the roots of her empathy for others evoked empathy within me for her and her loved ones, and for the suffering they endured. From that pain grew a powerful healer.

About halfway through the session, I felt my emotions break through. Tears in the beginning stages of crying welled up during a period of eye contact, and I pulled her close to me again. "Let it out," she said. It didn't last long, much like when it happens in therapy. It was a soft, breathy cry, not bawling, and I soon regained my composure. But there was some release.

*   *   *

I had a hard time shutting off my mind. The writer in me was making mental bookmarks of moments to remember so I could journal this experience, and I had to guard against writing it in my head before it had all unfolded. I got better at that in time. Late in the session she said I was more relaxed, more in the moment, and letting go more than I had been — "now that you're not interviewing me," she said, smiling and laughing softly. Indeed, I struggled with being fully in the moment, but part of that is an occupational hazard of being a writer.

The session became a series of back-and-forths — eye contact, followed by the tight hug with no eye contact, and the same again and again. Over time, the periods of eye contact lengthened as I got more comfortable with them. But she again noted that eye contact was hard for me, and she said I was almost bipolar about it, which she later described as "flippy," a pronounced all-or-nothing quality. I told her she could not have hit the nail more squarely on the head with that insight. In therapy I often describe myself as all or nothing.

Physically, it's hard for me to stay in the same position for very long, so we changed positions a few times. Late in the hour, she "squashed" me, curling up half against my left side and half on top of me. Again I could feel her strength and her positive energy. She had a way of making me forget how I was so much larger than she is, and that was more liberating than you probably can imagine.

After she left, I felt lighter than I had in years, as if I'd unloaded the weight of my world from my shoulders, and even my insides felt less stressed than I'd thought possible. My cravings — the ones that are my demons, always squeezing me in their tight grip — were gone. It was almost uncomfortable, this feeling of needing nothing to fill my emptiness. It was not the norm. It was beyond my ability to describe in words. In those moments, though, I dictated notes to myself so I could remember them later:

"Incredible. I have this feeling right now I haven't felt in a long time. I don't feel the heaviness of my body. I don't feel this big hole that needs to be filled."

It didn't last. In fact, it scared me, and within hours I sought comfort in food, in distraction, in my devices. The unbearable lightness of lightness, as I decided to call it, was too much for me. But it opened a door, giving me a chance to know it's possible to feel that way. It made me want to feel it again and to be able to let myself continue to feel it.

Sam has big plans for her cuddling business, which has drawn a lot of attention and has more demand than she can meet by herself. She's identified a building for a home base. She's going through applications from people who want to work with her and do what she does. She has a 40-hour training program designed for them. She's written a book. She's receiving hundreds of emails a day. I hope she's taking care of herself and doesn't burn out, and that as her cuddle business grows, it never strays from its simple roots: her caring soul.

The eye contact reminded me of *Marina Abramovic: The Artist is Present*, the powerful HBO documentary about the performance artist and her uncanny ability to be in the moment, and the effect she has on people who sit across from her and make eye contact with her. I recommended Sam see the documentary. I plan to watch it again after having cuddled with Sam.

Sam loves people. She has a way of drawing you out of your shell as she holds onto it. She has become part of a reawakening within

me, which someone else has been a big part of as well, a reawakening that's reminding me of what I want. Having stripped away all of my confusing cravings, all of the curiosities and fantasies that have overwhelmed me for so long, through touch I reconnected with who I am deep down, and what I want: a woman to share my life with, all of it — the confusion, the curiosities, the heaviness and the lightness, and all that's between them.

Between the first writing of this piece and the final edit, life happened, life continued, giving me insight that wasn't there in the days after Sam cuddled with me. Initially I thought there was something missing during the cuddle session: that my heart was not involved. In the early stages of attraction to someone else, I felt my heart was in another room, far away, but that it let me know it wants to be a part of physical touch, of cuddling, of intimacy, of my sexuality. It wants me to reclaim my whole self, not fragmented pieces that seem like the perfect fix at a certain moment. It wants me to learn how to integrate all of my pieces so I can love again, starting with loving myself.

That other person is no longer in my life, but I see now that in her own way she helped me reconnect with that aspect of my heart. She and Sam, in different ways, triggered moments of emotional catharsis connected to my heart, beginning the healing process. That connection was ephemeral, and I see that the journey will take a long time to complete, but I was given a glimpse of the future of my heart, and now I am moving step by step toward it.

At the end of the session, Sam gave me a choice. We would play a two-minute game — what she called "the repeat game," or eye contact. I would either try to make eye contact with her for two minutes, or for two minutes I would repeat a mantra she'd picked out for me and this session.

I chose the repeat game. So, for two minutes, I repeated each of the following sentences after she said them, all while making eye contact with her: "I am respected. I am accepted. I am worthy."

Thank you, Sam.

Sam told me when we met at the coffee shop two weeks earlier that her wish is for the world to evolve into a place where her service is no longer required. I don't see that happening anytime soon. In fact, I see the next piece of the new wave of alternative health care forming.

I'm wondering if others, especially men, feel some reluctance regarding contacting Sam for a cuddle. Is it somewhere on the scale of social stigma between 'Signing up for an online dating service' and 'Paying for sex?' Like, I want this, I need this, but I can't tell anyone I'm doing this? I've read comments at the bottom of news stories about Sam, and I am not surprised by the skepticism, the snark, the dismissal of her as someone using a gimmick to gain fame or fortune, or both. Others can evaluate her as they see fit. All I can speak to with any authority is how it felt to hold her for an hour, and for her to hold me, and to look into her eyes, and to feel my walls coming down.

The next day, when I learned my blood pressure was at its lowest in a long time, I couldn't help thinking I'd experienced the early stages of what will soon be considered an integral part of healing. I have little doubt that if in years from now massages are still covered by insurance plans, cuddling will be too. In fact, I am going to share this with my doctor.

But I wanted you to be the first to know.

And now you can share this story with the women in your life, women who might have a hard time believing that a man would pay someone to cuddle with him. I did, and it's one of the best things I've ever done for myself.

From Ivy League Lawyer to Porn Star

by Ben Peck

At 35 years old, I've found my true calling.

It is so far from the traditions of my family that none of us could have imagined it. My father was an engineer, my mother an administrator. I played with toy soldiers and models cars as a child, studied languages and literature in college, trained as an attorney and even served as a judge.

Yet today, I create and perform in feminist porn.

I grew up in very comfortable circumstances in Mystic, Connecticut, with two loving parents of Northern European Protestant ancestry who graced me with a doting childhood. They taught me I could do anything I wanted as long as I was a good student, so I made academic excellence the focus of my early life. They also taught me to be true to myself, and never to bear ill-will or malice. For them, and ultimately for me, life was about having just intentions above all else.

I never gave much thought to the world beyond school; in my primitive understanding, I believed that everything would simply fall into place if I got good grades, so I got good grades. I got into Columbia. I relished learning and looked upon my education as a means to make myself a well-rounded person, not as a means to churn out money for a corporation like many of my colleagues.

I studied subjects to which I felt naturally drawn. I learned German and Russian. I studied those nations' literature in their respective languages, along with philosophy, history and political theory. My time at Columbia radicalized my thinking. Among the principles that were sharpened during those years was compassion for the needy, a recognition of unfair power relationships in the world, and a pledge to combat injustice whenever possible.

I was radicalized sexually as well.

Growing up in Connecticut, I was a well-behaved, preppy boy. I wore button down shirts, khakis, and usually went to bed by 9:30 p.m. My sexual inclinations focused exclusively on girls. But within weeks of arriving in New York, I had dropped my khakis for baggy jeans, and rarely got to bed before 3 a.m. And after several sexual explorations with girls in my class, I discovered I had desires for boys, too.

In early 1999, I left New York to spend my junior year in Berlin. I lived with a remarkably generous guest family in the Schöneberg District. I perfected my German and fell into a lifestyle more sympathetic to my values than the one I had been living thus far.

Most Europeans I met seemed more interested in self-improvement than professional ambition and money. No one ever asked 'what I did.' Instead, they wanted to find out 'who I was,' what drove me, a question for which I had no answer when I first arrived in Berlin.

Still fresh out of adolescence, I became enthralled with Berlin's culture, especially its

> *But then, in the way things often happen, someone came into my life who completely helped to transform it.*

permissive night life. I haunted gay bars and clubs, discovering my sexual appetite in ways that would not have been possible for me in the U.S. I gradually became comfortable with my sexuality and grew to enjoy sex for its own sake. The more I embraced my desires, the more complete I felt in myself.

When I returned to New York late in 1999, I fell into a depression. My experience in Berlin had so revolutionized my outlook and so confirmed my deepest personal desires that I had difficulty readjusting to college life. I struggled through my final year of school, feeling alienated and alone.

When I left Columbia at age 22, I had a degree in Comparative Literature, cum laude, without any plan whatsoever. My first thought was to return to Germany.

But then, in the way things often happen, someone came into my life who completely helped to transform it.

Steve was 44. He was short, muscular, dark, and sensuous – a gypsy by blood, with a shaved head. I was tall, blond, lanky, and funky, my hair nearly down to the small of my back. Steve was charismatic, and I was drawn to him immediately. He seemed to know everyone and everything about New York, especially its gay scene in which I was still a novice.

From the start, our relationship was intensely physical but never monogamous. We shared the belief that sex was entertainment, to be enjoyed with as many people as possible. In clubs, at parties and at home, Steve enjoyed directing the action, especially with me, telling me what positions to take, how long to fuck, what to say, how to say it. I had already discovered in Berlin that I enjoyed the role of sexual showman. Performing for Steve deeply reso-

nated with me and through it, my sexual prowess grew.

Beyond sexual adventurer, Steve had a lot to give me at the time. He was worldly, shrewd, and experienced in business, while I was cerebral, theoretical, and impractical. He had been a film producer and a modeling agent with a huge rolodex. He always had money. He was brassy and fluent. He admired my intellectual capabilities and respected what I valued. He invited me to live with him in late 2000. I gladly accepted. To my own surprise, I had fallen in love with him.

Though I felt uncomfortable with his financial support, I had no way to make a living with the skills I had learned at Columbia. Steve encouraged me to reflect on this, and I thought deeply about it for some time.

After considering many possibilities, I decided I would commit myself to studying law. I believed the law was a force for good, and that it would somehow fulfill both my ethical and economic needs. Steve supported me unwaveringly in my decision.

In 2003, I began law school. I lost myself in the intellectual rigor, drinking up knowledge from all over. Although the courses were harder than anything I had previously encountered, I was more than up to the challenge because I had committed myself body and soul to the purpose. I completely changed my lifestyle to achieve academic excellence.

Throughout this time, my relationship with Steve flourished. Our sexual adventures never abated. My confidence as a sexual performer grew even stronger during law school. Steve and I often went to sex parties, clubs, and bathhouses in Chicago where we had moved so I could attend school. By day, I studied hard and trained rigorously at the gym. At night, I put my sexual abilities on full display, eventually earning a reputation as "finely tuned sex machine."

At the same time, my intellectual confidence grew. As I moved through law school, I discovered that it resonated with my deepest ethical instincts. I held to the idea that law could be an instrument for greater justice in society. If I could use my education to serve such ideals, I could accomplish something truly great.

In early 2006, just as my final semester in law school began, my father came down with pancreatic cancer. I had had no experience with death in my immediate family, and I refused to accept that he was dying. I was too preoccupied with my courses and my preparations for the Bar Exam to consider that my father, only 58, would die.

Gratefully, he saw me graduate in May. I began my Bar Exam studies the same month. He died on June 20th. I passed the Bar Exam on July 26th. I began working at a law firm ten days after passing the Bar Exam. I had no time to deeply grieve.

With my father's death, what once seemed so certain unwittingly came into question. "What does it matter whether I have a career when everything can end so quickly? What have I been ignoring in all these years of narrow study? What does all this flailing about for financial success really mean? It's all so superficial, so blind to real concerns, real experiences, real suffering."

Still, I found myself shackled with roughly $100,000 in student loans, and no law firms which specialized in what I loved and hoped to pursue: Constitutional Law. Instead, I felt forced to settle on a job as a trial lawyer for injury cases. I reasoned, if I couldn't serve the greater public good by using my legal education, then at least I could succor the injured in their quest for justice against those who harmed them.

But studying law and practicing it proved to be a different story. It quickly became apparent that my colleagues were exploiting the suffering of injured clients as a means to satisfy their own avarice. It was standard practice to use any methods necessary to wrest, cajole, or hack a settlement from anyone they sued. After all, if they won a case, my colleagues received a hefty one-third of the settlement. For them the law was a self-serving instrument to be wielded for "victory." The principles of law I so deeply valued were routinely violated. I quickly grew disillusioned.

After a year, I had seen enough. I fell into a moral crisis. Finally, I sat down with Steve and said, "I can't do this anymore." He told me that he understood, and with his support I quit practice on New Year's Eve. I felt confident that I would find a new path more consistent with my values.

I was happier in the months that followed. During this time I began to make sense of my father's death and his profound influence in shaping my life. It was he who taught me to value authenticity, fairness, and self-respect. I found consolation in knowing he would have been proud of my decision to leave my law practice.

> *For them the law was a self-serving instrument to be wielded for "victory." The principles of law I so deeply valued were routinely violated.*

But, like with most things in life, my sense of well-being did not last. Tragedy struck out of the blue.

One summer evening, Steve was recovering from a workout in the steam room when the pipes suddenly burst. The force of the explosion was so severe that he was thrown from the wood bench onto the floor where he lay amidst pools of boiling water for over 20 minutes. His body was seriously burned, his right arm so disfigured as to make it almost unrecognizable. He spent 35 days in the hospital suspended between life and death. He came close to death more than once.

His recovery was perilously slow. For months I sat at his bedside, dressed his wounds, managed his medical care, administered his medication, brought him food. As time passed, it became clear that he would be permanently disabled.

As the reality of this sank in, Steve spiraled into depression. In August 2009, two years after the accident, he suffered a complete mental collapse, landing in the psychiatric hospital with bipolar mania.

When he returned home months later, he was anxious whenever I left the house for even a few minutes. In my effort to keep him comfortable and sane, I became increasingly isolated and withdrawn. I felt I could not work even if I wanted to. And though I grew tired and weary, my loyalty never wavered.

Throughout this period of caregiving, my one respite was daily workouts at the gym, which I insisted on maintaining. I found satisfaction in the hard work and discipline it took to keep my body as finely tuned as ever. Although I generally stayed focused on my workouts, the occasional conversations that took place there provided something of a social outlet.

*　　*　　*

Once, a friend, who knew my circumstance, half-jokingly suggested that I place an ad online as an escort. Although the idea had not occurred to me, it instantly made sense. I could pay down my student loans and still spend most of my time attending to Steve. I had plenty of experience in "performance sex," and despite my recent abstinence, I had great confidence in my sexual abilities. The idea of men paying me for my attention excited me. It meshed with my desire for adoration which I had long ago eroticized.

Encouraged, I took a few naked pictures and put up an ad on Rentboy.com. I carefully described what I was willing and not willing to do. I immediately got calls from interesting men: Broadway directors, lawyers, Upper East Side bankers and travelers. And while I didn't find any of them especially attractive, after several years of almost no sex and the opportunity to be greatly admired, I was happy to see all of them.

I loved performing as an escort. My confidence grew steadily as I acquired repeat clients, all of whom strongly appreciated me. I soaked up the adoration, enjoyed exhibiting my body and its expressions of sexual agility. After years of feeling helpless with Steve, I felt empowered and, as importantly, fulfilled by satisfying my clients' sexual desires.

Few clients wanted vanilla sex. Because I was non-judgmental and respectful, clients felt safe to share their true desires. None of their requests seemed strange to me. Whether they wanted to be beaten or bound, made love to or pissed on, their desires were pure and honest. It satisfied me to gratify them.

But what thrilled me most was the idea that spending time with me actually positively affected my clients' lives. It wasn't just about sex. It was about connection, authenticity, healing. Through our conversations and play, clients learned to understand and honor what deeply aroused them. Many rediscovered parts of themselves that had long been repressed or buried; some even gained insight as to why. One client, whose partner of 30 years had died, told me that his time with me stopped him from committing suicide. Another chose me to bring sex back into his life for the first time since his true love was killed in 1971.

My confidence grew steadily as I acquired repeat clients, all of whom strongly appreciated me. I soaked up the adoration, enjoyed exhibiting my body and its expressions of sexual agility.

The skills that I had learned in caring for Steve translated into my work as an escort. At times, I considered myself as much of a healer as any therapist.

And I was healing myself, too, discovering the many facets of who I was through each new experience.

Because I loved to be admired not just for my body, but for the satisfaction I could bring to others, it occurred to me that video might be another way to accomplish what I increasingly felt was my purpose.

Showing off for the camera proved immensely exciting, especially since I could stay rock hard and shoot tremendous ejaculations. With the same seriousness I applied to my law studies, I tailored my diet and trained my penis muscles to make sure I performed at peak capacity. I posted dozens of solo jerk-off videos on Xtube.com, where I won an army of fans. I felt intoxicated by making porn that not only brought pleasure to people, but also helped them to understand who they were.

I also felt proud. I was finally carving out a more authentic life, including fully honoring my commitment to Steve. For the first time in many years, life was lighter and happier. Although I carried the same burdens, I was bearing them with a sense that there was something there for me too.

Other fascinating things happened. The more I allowed myself to express my true desires, the more they shifted and changed. Increasingly, my fantasies turned toward women. When I watched porn, all of it was straight. After 12 years of absence, women returned to my fantasies and dreams, and then to my life

Straight porn is my current frontier. Unfortunately, most of what I've viewed of commercial porn promotes a male-centered vision of desire in which men are always erect and women are ever-ready to serve their needs. It is vision that has led to cartoonish portrayals of beauty, misogyny, and, in many cases, female exploitation.

Porn can accomplish greater psychological and social good if it becomes more "feminist." Rather than focusing on men getting off, it can include the complete human sexual experience: intimacy, respect for difference and varying desire, respectful and loving interchange between the genders, and the mutual pursuit of pleasure; and especially, an account of female desires.

To this end I am now creating and performing in videos that I hope will revolutionize pornography.

It has been nearly three years since I began escorting, and nearly as long since taping my first porn video. I recently stopped accepting new escorting clients, preferring instead to spend time with longtime ones with whom I have developed deep friendships. These are authentic relationships which are maintained by trust, and they continue to bring meaning and satisfaction into all of our lives.

Through all of these experiences, I have fiercely held on to the ideals of honor and self-respect which I inherited from my parents. Conventional morality has had no place in my life. Against it, I have explored every corner of sexuality and have seen firsthand the healing power of sex and the tremendous contribution it can make to our sense of well-being.

Positive sex is beautiful sex. What could be hotter than following our own truth?

Curing Pornophobia: How Watching Pornography Can Change Your Life

by Stanley Siegel

The great majority of us around the world watch pornography. Nearly 87 percent of men and 76 percent of women reportedly visit adult entertainment websites. In fact, pornography drives the economy of the Internet and our appetite for it has led to Internet innovation.

That sex sells is hardly a startling discovery. However, what attracts us to pornography, and why as a culture we demonize it, might be.

Ideally, sex creates a moment of extreme intensity, an altered state of consciousness, in which the past and present, body, mind and spirit all merge to form a new reality, unlike most other experiences in our lives.

But what most of us don't acknowledge is that our private fantasies during sex are often more exciting than what we are actually physically doing. Self-styled pornography is constantly running in our head. We focus on the images, thoughts, or stories from our imagination that truly arouse us, especially when our true desires are not aligned with the experience at hand. It's our dirty little secret: Our hidden fantasies are what actually make us climax.

Sexual fantasies are a near-universal experience. Whether they are long, drawn-out scenarios or a quick flash of imagery, they are far from random imaginings. The stories and images that excite us onscreen, from romance to bondage scenes, are visual representations of our deeper truth, which is why pornography is so compelling. When we watch it, we are accessing the details of our own fantasies, even those that may not have been in our consciousness until then.

And if we dig even deeper into our unconscious, we will discover at the base of these fantasies fragments of our personal history and conflicts that lead far back into our repressed past. No one leaves childhood without some conflict of unmet need. For most of us, the pain or unhappiness associated with these conflicts does not preoccupy our current thoughts and feelings, but does become part of our individual psychology, setting the stage for how we interact with the world.

At some point during the heightened sexuality of adolescence, we unconsciously eroticize these unmet needs or unresolved conflicts from childhood in a complicated attempt to heal ourselves. In other words, we turn those painful experiences into pleasurable ones to counteract their power over us.

As we grow into adulthood, these same conflicts (which now have sexual themes) are coded in our fantasies and desires. Through our sexuality, we attempt to gain mastery over our feelings of powerlessness, shame, guilt, fear, and loneliness that might otherwise defeat us.

If we learn to identify and understand our fantasies, we can use them to create sexual experiences that are more aligned with our true desires by intentionally choosing partners with whom we are sexually compatible. If we can go even a step further still: by decoding what these desires detail about our past, we can use that knowledge to heal the conflicts that originally gave rise to them. Understanding our sexual fantasies is a key to understanding who we are.

*   *   *

Pornography access is easy. All it requires is an Internet connection. It doesn't take much time or emotional involvement with others. The Internet has made exploring our sexual fantasies more accessible. We can use the extensive offerings and variations of pornography, interactive role-play, fantasy chat rooms, and other forms of eroticized communication to explore our deepest desires. The Internet collaborates non-threateningly with the secretiveness which cloaks our inner, private fantasies.

By becoming the characters in pornography, we discover the themes that truly turn us on. Do we identify with the master or slave, the romantic hero or villain? Are we excited by spanking, ropes, or handcuffs? Do we like forceful or tender love-making? What porn site do we keep returning to? What scene do we continually replay? None of this is as random as it seems. It's all a window into our inner lives.

Pornography is often condemned and legally restricted, even banned, though never suppressed successfully.

Why? Because pornography speaks to the deepest level of sexuality. We are unable to repress the truth. Porn doesn't corrupt our thoughts, it provides a direct link to them. It's a source of enlightenment.

> *...what most of us don't acknowledge is that our private fantasies during sex are often more exciting than what we are actually physically doing. Self-styled pornography is constantly running in our head.*

Pornography does not make its consumers sexually aggressive or foster sexism. In fact, exposure to pornography might make some people less likely to commit sexual crimes. Some surveys suggest that viewing porn leads to increased frequency of actual sex, but not to sex outside of given relationships.

Recently, in a *Playboy* radio interview, a caller asked me if I could explain his wife's fantasies and what he should do about them. He described her as sexually frigid. "She never seems to really like sex," he said. But recently she had confessed to him, after secretly watching an online video, that she had fantasized dressing in a nun's habit and being "forcibly taken."

I told the caller that fantasies of forced sex were common among women because of social training, since many women don't feel entitled to enjoy sex and are taught to feel guilty if they do.

"What could be more symbolic of such purity than a nun's habit?" I asked.

In a fantasy of forced sex such as his wife's, I explained, his wife was shedding responsibility for her desire and therefore didn't have to feel guilty or ashamed for enjoying it.

Furthermore, it was flattering to her that a man was so overwhelmed by desire for her that he couldn't control himself despite the prohibition the religious garb symbolized.

"Oh, I get it," the caller said. "She comes from a very strict upbringing." Then, after a moment, "Is it wrong to have sex with her that way?" I asked him what would be wrong about it. He said that while he too fantasized acting aggressively toward her, he was afraid his wife would lose respect for him or maybe even herself. "There may be that risk," I replied, "but the potential benefit is that it might be the first time your wife feels sexually free enough to let go. The experience could lead to a new understanding of herself and a smarter sex life for both of you."

I also suggested that guided by their newly found openness, they might consider surfing Internet sex sites together. Some experts say that our brains do need novelty, but also that by frequently viewing porn we will incur a tendency toward sexual compulsiveness.

However, I disagree.

Every compulsion has a healthy intention. We reenact rituals in an effort to soothe pain and conflict. The key to unhooking ourselves from compulsively seeking porn is not going cold turkey, as counselors often advise. It's to use the pornography to identify our true desires and where they come from and then use that knowledge to guide us to a partner with whom we are sexually and otherwise compatible. When we use porn to figure this out, the need to compulsively consume it will disappear because our fantasy and sex lives have merged and sex has become meaningful and satisfying.

Critics say by watching porn we are committing an act of unfaithfulness to our partners. But unless we know who we are sexually, that is until our mind and spirit are aligned with our sexual behavior, we remain unfaithful to ourselves and can never be truly faithful to anyone, because the stories in our head will continue to dominate our sexual experience and alienate us from our lover. Porn does not separate sex from emotion; our lack of understanding of who we are, does.

Do we identify with the master or slave, the romantic hero or villain?

*　　*　　*

In business, my patient Scott earned a reputation as a brilliant deal maker. A skilled corporate lawyer, he was considered highly intelligent and shrewd, indeed, ruthless. By the time he came to see me, those who cared about him felt he was, "out of control." Winning a deal had become more important to him than anything else in his life. To his friends, he had grown arrogant and to his competitors, "a terrible sore loser."

At about five-foot-five, Scott was a short man with a wiry frame and sharp features. Always the smallest in his class and not particularly athletic, he felt like an outsider growing up.

From the time he first discovered sex, Scott had fantasized about large breasts. In fact, he had fetishized them. The bigger the better. He imagined himself nestled between them, his lips and tongue languishing on one, then the next. As a young man, he spent countless hours on sites of big-breasted women. When a scene "clicked," he masturbated to its images. He confessed to me early on that at those moments when he climaxed, he felt small and safe, a feeling that he would never indulge otherwise.

During his therapy Scott's story slowly unfolded. He was raised in southern California by a mother who was more demanding than nurturing, who constantly berated his father for his career failures. She imagined a better life for herself and Scott and later depended on Scott to provide for her in ways in which her husband had disappointed her. She regularly told Scott: "Your father is weak. People always take advantage of him. He's a loser." And while Scott adored his father for his kindness and affection, he agreed with his mother's assessment.

Feeling his size and background were a disadvantage, and believing that his father wasn't much of a man, Scott set out to become the man that he wished his father had been. He fought against his feelings of inferiority by approaching his life with purpose and discipline that drove him to the front of the class. Now, at 32, no one could ever say that Scott wasn't a man. He had achieved success, had enough money and a list of clients that other lawyers envied.

Of course, he was as driven sexually as much as he was with work, though he hadn't met with as much romantic success. While some women were attracted to his money and position, most were disappointed with his performance in bed. He didn't have the equipment or prowess to measure up to his promise. In fact, much to the dismay of more than one woman, Scott only wanted to spend hours nursing on their breasts. Through our conversations, Scott recognized the symbolic meaning of his breast fantasies. Despite his bravura, he had always felt small, weak, and inadequate, and he had long ago eroticized these feelings in what was an unconscious attempt to heal from his fear of turning out like his father. With their capacity to nurture, breasts could strengthen and fortify him as well as make him feel safe.

As Scott learned more about what drove his sense of inadequacy and dealt with it in therapy, he also sought out more directly what he needed in his relationships with women. His aggressive behavior softened. And while large breasts continued to appeal to him, he didn't attach the same meaning to them. Over time, his sexual repertoire expanded as he understood that his deeper needs could be gratified in situations with women that were based on respect, generosity, and trust. And although his penis didn't grow, his self-worth did and he became a better lover.

A Dangerous Method:
Can Sex Restore Mental Health?

by Stanley Siegel

The film *A Dangerous Method* tells the story of the complex relationship between Sigmund Freud and his much younger heir-apparent, Carl Jung, both early founders of the modern field of psychology. Freud and Jung came to represent differing schools of psychoanalytic thinking, a separation not only hastened by intellectual disagreements but by a rupture in their friendship over the married Jung's sexual relationship with his patient, Sabina Spielrein. Through this Oedipal drama we witness the emergence of a way of understanding human nature that first shocked the world and now, a century later, dominates our thinking.

Like psychoanalysis itself, the movie explores ideas about sexuality, especially the tension between the anarchy of desire and the necessity for its confinements.

It begins when young Spielrein is committed to Jung's Switzerland clinic for treatment for hysteria. His first psychoanalytic patient, Jung and Spielrein engage in an intellectual and emotional expedition of what was then uncharted territory, the subconscious. Through Jung's uncovering questioning, Sabina slowly recalls episodes from her embattled childhood, reliving the feelings that traumatized her.

By conferring with fellow analyst Otto Gross, a libertine sent by Freud for treatment, Jung finds the rationale for entering into a sexual relationship with Spielrein, whom he has barely resisted. He convincingly argues that effective treatment requires more than Freud's "talking cure." A proponent of sexual emancipation, Gross considers all repression an artifact of another era, making the case that sex with patients is both a moral and therapeutic imperative. That's all that Jung needs to begin a sexual relationship with Sabina as part of her treatment.

The filmmakers stay faithful to representing the shifting values and mores of this nascent period of early psychology and do not judge Jung's affair by contemporary standards. Instead, they present the transgression of the doctor-patient boundary – an established treatment protocol yet to be formed – as emotionally fraught, yet deeply therapeutic in restoring Speilrein's mental health.

Jung's approach is radical by any standard. He recreated the childhood beatings Spielrein endured from her abusive father. By helping her understand her pain in the consultation room and fully experiencing the childhood trauma that she has come to eroticize in the bedroom, she is slowly restored to health.

The treatment is not a one-way street. Spielrein not only plays a major role in the intellectual development of Jung's theories, she also helps him face his own repressed sexuality, though the film never gives the details.

Increasingly conflicted emotionally and professionally by the betrayal of his wife, Emma, Jung breaks off his relationship with Spielrein. He also breaks with Freud over his interest in spirituality and mysticism.

Spielrein leaves Switzerland to study medicine and eventually becomes an influential psychoanalyst.

*　　*　　*

In the hundred years since, we've learned a great deal about the consequences of violating doctor-patient boundaries and developed a strict code of ethics for protecting the sanctity of the therapeutic relationship. Some of the ideas that were explored in the early experiments of psychoanalysis have been discarded, while others have had a profound impact on contemporary therapies.

Expanding on accepted theories of sexuality in my book, *Your Brain on Sex*, I explain how during the heightened sexuality of adolescence, we eroticize unmet childhood needs and unresolved conflicts in a complicated attempt to heal ourselves. In other words, we turn early painful experiences into pleasurable ones in order to counteract their power over us. As we grow into adulthood, these same conflicts, which now have sexual themes, are encoded in our fantasies and desires, or in some cases, in our sexual behavior. Through our sexuality, we attempt to gain mastery over feelings of powerlessness, shame, guilt, fear, and loneliness that might otherwise defeat us.

While I do not condone Jung's relationship with Spielrein or sex between any therapist and patient, I do espouse acting out sexual desire within the context of what I call a "restorative" experience that can have powerful therapeutic potential.

In restorative experiences with our partner, through safe and consensual measures, we bring to life our deepest and most eroticized desires, acting out fantasies whose symbolic meaning in metaphor we have already come to revere.

Whether the scenario is as conventional as romantic seduction, or as unconventional as extreme bondage, we connect – physically, emotionally, and spiritually – with the deepest part of our psyches, recovering what was suppressed or lost. In the process, we restore ourselves to wholeness.

Of course, the deepest and most lasting healing comes when we have the opportunity to experience our true desires and work through the mastery of the conflicts behind them over time. Whether it's with a lover or spouse, a restorative relationship assumes an emotional posture that is often diametrically opposite from the dysfunctional ones we experienced in our childhood. Characterized by openness, intimacy, and mutual respect, the new relationship allows us to derive a new settlement to old conflicts. Within this friendship, sex is not separated from the joys and struggles of daily life, nor diminished by its challenges. Instead it offers a rich and fertile ground for a meaningful and satisfying life.

Nearly two years after his divorce, Jason came to see me for a consultation. Tall, handsome, 45 years old with deep blue eyes and a shock of gray hair, Jason was having problems with women. He had no trouble meeting them, but he found that after dating for a few months, they would invariably end the relationship.

When I asked him why, he said, "Women think I'm too laid back. I get called things like passive or dull. They lose their patience or get bored. They yawn in my face."

By the time he'd come to see me, Jason had given up dating and was spending his free time in his workshop repairing old watches, avoiding the world. But after a good friend approached Jason and got him to confess that he was depressed over his relationships with women, he agreed to seek therapy.

Shy and soft-spoken, Jason grew up as the scion of a privileged New England family known for its wealth, as well as its lack of accomplishments. Although Jason's father was an architect, he had never been successful. Instead, he enjoyed time on the golf course at the same club to which his own father and grandfather had belonged.

Jason informed me early on that he was "proud to be a terrible disappointment to my parents." When I asked him how he'd disappointed them, he replied, "Because I refused to follow the social agenda they set for me." Instead, he had devoted himself to more intellectual pursuits repairing watches, even owning a small repair shop. When he wasn't being "totally ignored by his father," Jason said, he was being berated by him for his disloyalty to family tradition, a label Jason wore like a badge. Jason's mother, whom he described as cold, put most of her energy into fundraising for local charities. "Everything for strangers, nothing for family," Jason said.

Although Jason told me that he'd rejected his family's social expectations, he nonetheless found himself dating woman from his same social class. "In general," he said, "they turned out to be more like my parents than not. And mostly they choose me."

While it seemed obvious that Jason's depression was related to his long-standing conflict with his parents, I chose to approach it by first examining his failure with women, the symptom that had brought him to therapy.

When we began to talk about chemistry, Jason seemed puzzled by the concept. "It's not something that's ever happened on my end,"

Characterized by openness, intimacy, and mutual respect, the new relationship allows us to derive a new settlement to old conflicts.

he said. When I asked why, he insisted he had no idea. When finally pushed to explore what might attract him, he imagined a woman with "a kind, open face, delicate features and a sweet disposition, nothing like the women I've gone out with." This seemed to come as a surprise.

As the therapy unfolded and Jason grew more comfortable exploring his sexual fantasies, he came to understand that what actually aroused him was the image of being gently caressed. He craved tenderness – "soft kisses and gentle fondling." In the past, when he engaged in sex with woman, his orgasms came prematurely or not at all, disappointing everyone. Now, when he brought himself to orgasm, he imagined "the gentle touch of fingers brushing against my back." Jason soon recognized that he had unknowingly sexualized the qualities that he had so long ago craved from his parents – warmth and tenderness.

It was clear how his lack of authenticity had contributed to his failures. In his past sexual practice, he had never experienced such feelings because the women who had chosen him were cold, no match for what he now recognized as his true desires. Caught up in his rebellion against his parents, he had sabotaged his chance at happiness by engaging women who resembled them and whom he would then punish by withdrawing until they gave up.

Once Jason understood this, he decided he could break the cycle and search for an experience in which he could honor his true sexual desires. For the first time, he felt excited about dating. He posted a profile on a popular Internet dating site which included a brief and poetic description of his sexual interests and within a short time received a dozen well-suited responses.

Within a few months Jason had met a woman whom he described as lovely. And as shy as he was, Jason took my advice and began to talk about sex after a handful of dates. He opened the conversation by speaking about his own experiences, and then gently worked toward asking about hers. By then the conversation seemed natural. They quickly discovered that they felt the same way about sex – they were both turned on by the gentle touching and tenderness. It wasn't long before they were having sex.

"This was the first time I actually made love," Jason told me, "and it was tender and beautiful. I find myself wanting to be generous with her in every way and for hours. She asks nothing of me, expects nothing from me. She comes from a middle-class family, the sort my parents wouldn't have talked to. But I've met them also, and they're as kind as she is. I've finally realized that being in a family doesn't have to mean being in a prison."

Jason had broken the cycle. By following the steps of *Intelligent Lust* he discovered his true sexual nature, then succeeded at choosing a partner with whom he was not only sexually compatible, but who enabled him to heal an old family conflict.

Forbidden Desire:
The Cost of Living Without Sex

by Stanley Siegel

Sexual denial never succeeds and sexual desire can never be buried.

Why do some of us choose to live without sex? What is the emotional cost of sexual abstinence to parts of our lives?

The secret life story of former FBI Director J. Edgar Hoover, a closeted gay man, told in the Clint Eastwood biopic, *J. Edgar*, tragically depicts how self-denial eroded his soul and how the projection of Hoover's self-hatred destroyed many other lives.

In my clinical experience, while religious or societal prohibitions account for why some people choose to forego sex, shame is the primary reason we starve ourselves of sexual pleasure. Hoover, a man deeply entangled with his fanatically controlling mother, as shown in the film, suppressed his homosexual desires rather than suffer her disdain. "I would rather have a dead son than a daffodil," she tells him.

In annihilating his sexuality, all while simultaneously conducting a lifetime campaign against "alien" influences on the nation as an architect of the communist "red scare," Hoover sought to cleanse a perceived dirtiness which haunted him.

When Hoover, at 29, took over what would become the FBI, during the Coolidge administration, he installed Clyde Tolson as his second-in-command, with whom he then carried on a chaste love affair until the day he dropped dead in his bedroom during the Nixon presidency. Enthralled with each other, Hoover and Tolson pledge to lunch and dine together daily. They join private country clubs, vacation at the horse track, and rub elbows with Hollywood celebrities on the red carpet, their meticulous appearance just so much armor cloaking their secret bond. Hoover's prospective marriage to the actress Dorothy Lamour results in a violent episode, with Tolson nearly walking out and Hoover desperately promising his aide to never abandon him and make him his heir.

Hoover's grandiosity stemmed from his early childhood. Powerless under his mother, he used his cunning to convert his helplessness and rage into an authoritarian fervor that allowed him to blackmail presidents and persecute his perceived enemies. Hoover's covert investigations of Eleanor Roosevelt's suspected love affair with a female journalist, John F. Kennedy's frequent sexual affairs, as well as Martin Luther King's sexual peccadilloes, made him untouchable.

As a result, no one dared to out Hoover. He thus achieved dominance over what he believed was the nation's moral chaos, and at the same time sublimated his own internal turmoil and the erotic secret behind it.

Sexual denial never succeeds and sexual desire can never be buried. Sexual truth always finds self-expression, whether in surreptitious acts or in its beholder's preoccupations. All kinds of sexual desires – not just homosexual ones – that people consider sinful or perverse undergo such internal policing, in large measure due to a self-image at war with itself. The male CEO who by day is the master of his corporation and who by night masturbates to domination fantasies – but will never

67

hire a dominatrix – is a man who is an impostor to himself.

Such patients wind up in therapy after their sexual self-denial takes a significant toll on their lives.

My patient Aaron, for example, worried about his lack of interest in sex. He even attributed his straight A's in college to avoiding sex.

But sex was not the reason Aaron thought he came to therapy. Exhaustion was. Despite sleeping eight hours nightly, in the mornings he awoke wrecked, often nodding off at his well-paid job as a network engineer.

After a physician ruled out a physical problem, I wondered if disturbing dreams were robbing Aaron of the rest he needed to live a normal life. His answer to my question was the key that began to open the door behind which he had so firmly locked his sexuality.

Aaron told me: "I usually read until I'm groggy, then I turn the light off. I'm dead out. The next thing I know, it's morning. The alarm rings and I can't open my eyes. I hit the snooze button and wake up when it goes off. I feel like I haven't slept at all."

After some continued, gentle questioning, Aaron disclosed that, sometimes, he did in fact wake up – albeit briefly,

"I never remember dreaming but I know I must," he said.

"How do you know?" I asked.

Aaron was silent for a moment before replying. "Because either I am jerking myself off in my sleep or I'm having wet dreams," he said with an embarrassed smile. "I'm sticky down there."

"So you may be having a whole other life when you're asleep," I said. "Do you have sex or masturbate at other times?"

"Not really. I don't have much of a sex drive."

"Well, apparently you do when you're sleeping," I replied and we both laughed.

It seemed obvious that Aaron had so thoroughly repressed his sexual desires that whatever was truly exciting to him must have seemed so unthinkable that he could not allow it to surface in his consciousness. The challenge became to discover what was behind his amnesia. I suggested that each night for a week, he set his alarm to wake him at different times, and with paper and pen handy, record what he dreamt.

He thus achieved dominance over what he believed was the nation's moral chaos, and at the same time sublimated his own internal turmoil and the erotic secret behind it.

He returned in a week with a journal in which he had written the following:

"Thursday 3 am: Dream. Feet. Beautifully sculpted, deep arches, soft gentle smell, natural toenails. Kissing them gently rubbing them, massaging them. Hard on. Lots of pre-cum. I am incredibly excited."

Then:

"Saturday 3:30 am. I'm sucking toes. No body or face attached. Just feet. Beautiful toes. I'm really hard. I rub my cock against the sole of the feet and start to fuck them. They grab my cock."

We sat in silence for a moment.

"How do you feel about what you discovered?" I gently asked.

For the first time Aaron felt safe enough to open up.

"A mixture of being freaked out – shame and relief. I mean, it wasn't a total shock to me. I remember having more than the usual interest in feet and shoes as a kid. I loved going to buy new shoes. I didn't know what it meant. But the whole feeling of the shoe store, watching people take their socks off, the smell, trying on shoes, measuring feet. I would drag my mother into any shoe store when we were out shopping.

"After a few times, she must have sensed something. She told me it was odd. We stopping buying shoes in stores. She would order them for me from catalogues. I'd hide the catalogues under my bed and read them at night. I didn't know why. I didn't know it was erotic, but I just couldn't wait to look at them. I also felt really ashamed. Later, in high school, when I took gym class, I tried not to look at the other kids' feet. At first, I couldn't resist, then after time and a lot of bargaining with God, I made myself stop thinking about it."

"You said you felt a combination of shame and relief."

"I feel like a freak. I'm turned on by feet. Not a pretty face or breasts. Feet. That's kind of humiliating."

"Why relief then?" I asked, maintaining a sincerely calm tone.

"I don't know. I think it's because at least I'm sexual. I think I was already feeling like a freak…because I had no interest in sex like every other guy in his twenties did. But, what happened to that sweet little kid who just so happened to love feet? It's so sad."

Aaron began to cry. I waited until he calmed himself and then told him stories of other patients and their true erotic desires – the young man who got excited whenever someone sneezed, the rabbi and Kaballah scholar who masturbated while thinking about women wearing eyeglasses. I talked about how our erotic desires had meaning and how we could together discover the poetry in the purpose of his fantasies.

Like Hoover, Aaron denied his sexual desires. He, too, came from a family of deeply controlling parents. Both suffered a form of alienation. Where homosexuality was dirty to Hoover, intimacy overwhelmed Aaron. Feet were preferable to engaging with a whole person.

Our sexual desires, in themselves, carry no real threat to our well-being. It's how we judge those desires that makes the difference between life-affirming action or soul-killing self-denial. The stories of people like Hoover and Aaron share the theme of shame. Aaron will likely transcend it and eventually find satisfaction in aligning his secret desires with authentic behavior. Sadly, J. Edgar Hoover had no such opportunity. The tyranny of shame had disastrous effects on his and the nation's life.

The Next Sexual Revolution

by Stanley Siegel

Can we ever have an honest conversation about sex? The phenomena we've veiled behind sacred secrecy and mystique? Our backstories, our fantasies, our partners, our surroundings and our societies at large have all played colossal roles in establishing our subjective desires – *subjective* being the crux of our erotica, here. Yet, as much as we consider our own desires to be a complex interaction of interpersonal satisfaction, we must also apply this compassionate curiosity to the sexual lives of others lest we be incompatibly prescribed the revered misassumptions of Hollywood and Madison Avenue.

Some of us think of sex as a simple act of physical pleasure, while for others it's a way of communicating deep feelings. Still others see sex as a spiritual experience. The definition of sexual activity also differs from person to person. It can be kissing, touching, intercourse, bondage, oral, conversational, punishing, dominating, wrapped in leather, romantic, observing, disciplining, and much, much more. It is as varied as our individual personalities.

Whatever our way of expressing it, sex creates a moment of extreme intensity in which our entire inner life — our history and imagination — is expressed in actions. It is an altered state of consciousness in which the past and the present, the body, mind and spirit, all merge to form a new reality unlike any other experience in our lives.

Why is it, then, that sex is so often physically and mentally ungratifying when it can divine such healing? Why does sex so often alienate us from ourselves and our partners when it has such potential to bring feelings of closeness and intimacy?

To answer this, we first need to understand the impact that social and cultural institutions have on how we think and feel about sex. Much of the way we each experience sex is shaped by what we learn through family attitudes and religious associations. Often, our true sexual desires conflict with these teachings, leading us to deny or suppress whole parts of ourselves.

As Americans, we have a complicated relationship with sex, simultaneously promoting "sexy" images in popular culture to sell products while demonizing those of us who enjoy it. Sometimes sex is portrayed as a romantic seduction in which it's used to win the man. Other times partners are shown tearing each other's clothes off and engaging in ravenous behavior, giving the impression that sex is primitive and instinctual and requires no thought.

Pornography, because it is so massively viewed, also plays a significant role in how we experience sex. Most pornography negatively objectifies female sexuality, perpetuating cultural notions of female desire driven by the need to gratify men. Men, too, are objectified. They are shown as always erect and ready to go. Porn promotes caricatures: Women with enormous breasts and men with big dicks, reducing sexual interaction to a form of adult cartoon. The object in current porn is the "money" shot — unenlightened consumption with no positive emotional interaction.

Our ideas about sex are also enshrined in our language. In English, for instance, the most commonly used verb denoting sexual intercourse is fuck. The word *fuck* shares roots with the German verb *ficken*, meaning "to rub harshly; scratch; itch; strike." It also shares roots with the Dutch verb *fokken*, meaning "to thrust," as well as the Swedish *focka*, meaning "to strike; kick; push." Unlike euphemisms such as "sex," "coitus," "make love," "copulate" and "lie with," fuck gets right to the conceptual point; it does not shy from the meaning of the activity it describes. Also ensconced in language are pernicious gender stereotypes, power inequality, and violence. Those who freely engage in sex are labeled "whores," "sluts," and "players."

Attitudes toward sex change slowly over time, but not without political and social intervention. Building on the sexual revolution of the 1960's which first brought sex into the national conversation, the feminist movements have redefined notions of female desire, correcting gender stereotypes and reinforcing pro-female principles of sexual entitlement and female-centric pleasure.

Feminism has not only pushed us to think more deeply about sexual objectification and exploitation; it has begun to help us parse out individualized ideas of sexuality. But even new labels that have emerged to describe sexuality as a result of social change, such as "gay," "bisexual," or "transgendered," typically fall short of encompassing the complexity of our true sexuality.

For most of us, the specifics of what we eroticize, that is, the thoughts, images, or sensations that trigger a climax, still remain bare-

> *Whatever our way of expressing it, sex creates a moment of extreme intensity in which our entire inner life — our history and imagination — is expressed in actions.*

ly understood. Reimagining sex in a new light requires us to not only grapple with the language, the popular images, and the politics of sex stereotyping, but it helps each of us to more deeply understand our specific desires, what they mean, and how to honor them. By recognizing the individual psychology behind our desires, namely, the individual expression of subjective desire — we can invent democratic models for sex that are based on authenticity, sensitivity, respect, and generosity. This next wave must wash away all negative conceptual relics that force us to define ourselves by mass-marketed labels.

Sexual politics has made few inroads into the powerful world of pornography. A billion dollar industry with cutting edge technology, pornography continues to perpetuate negative images of sex as violence and possession. Past strategies of condemning, censoring or ignoring have failed, and now they must be replaced by ones that aggressively appropriate pornography as an instrument for positive change.

Some radical women including Candida Royale, Anna Span, Petra Joy, and Tristan Taormino, and also a few men, are already creating a new kind of pornography that places sexual pleasure in a meaningful context.

Ben Peck is one mentioned activist, for instance, attempting to do that and more. After performing in porn for a few years, Peck has begun to produce, write, and appear in films that represent a total re-envisioning of the traditional form. "Let's face it," Peck says, "Porn is among the most successful financial industries. We have to use its vast power to produce sexual healing and transformation. Porn should be liberating and inspiring rather than oppressive."

Concerned over its effects, he seeks to offer a counterpoint to the depiction of male dominance as an acceptable form of "sexy sexism." Peck's porn presents an alternative to hardcore "fuck films." "Typically, men appear always hard and women ever ready to please them." Instead, Peck's men aim to satisfy their partner's desires rather than to simply get off; women expect to receive pleasure just as much as men.

Where most pornography creates an unreal universe, Peck's videos are closer to real situations, striking a visceral chord of recognition, while introducing new, exciting, or surprising possibilities for sexual engagement never seen in conventional porn. While all pornography is fantasy in the place of reality, Peck's work is nearer to documentary in that it seeks to educate and nourish rather than addict. These films translate people's true fantasies into honest, authentic scenarios on screen.

Peck turns porn on its head, creating relationships in which women are empowered sexually, and men are engaged and not threatened. "The fact is that men as much as women hunger for intimacy," says Peck. "Affirmation and intimacy are human needs. I want to provide the link between hot sex and intimacy that will satisfy both desires." Without sacrificing intensity or passion, Peck is more concerned with respect, mutual affirmation, and generosity than control and domination. Partners actually care for and adore each other. If domination is involved, it is based on mutual desire rather than oppression.

In contrast to one-dimensional themes and characters found in most porno, Peck's scripts have complex themes that allow viewers to identify, understand, and honor unexplored aspects of their sexuality, deepening their self-knowledge.

By identifying with specific images, characters, and their actions, viewers can pinpoint exactly what turns them on and what leads to climax. Do we identify with the character who is being admired, the one who is fucking or getting fucked, acts of tenderness, aggression, passion, or body contact? Peck's videos help us explore and define our sexuality for ourselves. When there is not a single image shoved down our throats, or no one shaming or judging us, that is what truly expresses us.

Peck's videos help us to intelligently explore and define our sexuality for ourselves, not according to one-dimensional stereotypes.

As a sexual radical, Peck thinks beyond traditional notions of sexual identity. He is equally erotically charged performing solo as he is with same- or opposite-sex partners. "Good sex requires the ability to be completely present in moments of tenderness, submission, romance, domination, intimacy, abandon, and self-adulation, connecting deeply with the self and with our partners, regardless of their gender. Breaking down sexual roles, categories and myths is a path to finding authenticity and wholeness.

Young people are increasingly more fluid in their sexuality, which lays the groundwork

By identifying with specific images, characters, and their actions, viewers can pinpoint exactly what turns them on and what leads to climax.

for our reimagined porn. I want to help viewers identify their true sexual desires, transcending socially constructed expectations."

Sex based on cultural stereotypes and mass-marketed images is alienating and unsatisfying because it supplants individual desire. The next revolution promises smarter, hotter sex based upon mutual affirmation, positive objectification, and an equal commitment to pleasure for all parties.

About the Authors

Stanley Siegel, LCSW

Stanley is a psychotherapist, author, lecturer, and former Director of Education and Senior Faculty member of New York's renowned Ackerman Institute for Family Therapy. With nearly 40 years of experience in the field of psychology, Stanley has developed a bold and unconventional approach to psychotherapy that has led to his most recent book, *Your Brain on Sex: How Smarter Sex Can Change Your Life*. Siegel has taught at the State University of New York at Stony Brook, Adelphi University, and the University of California, Berkeley. Additionally, he was the founding director of the Family Studies Center in Huntington, NY, and has served as a consultant to hospitals and mental health centers throughout the country.

The creator and writer of the "Families" column for *Newsday*, Siegel also co-authored two popular books: *The Patient Who Cured His Therapist and Other Unconventional Stories of Therapy* and *Uncharted Lives: Understanding the Life Passages of Gay Men*, both of which have been translated into 6 languages. His books serve as the basis for workshops around the country. Siegel has served as the review editor for two professional marital therapy journals, and his work with couples and families is the subject of two educational videos.

Siegel's lifelong interest in art has included a period during the mid-1990s as the Dance Editor for *Showbusiness*, in which he reviewed and reported on the dance scene in New York City. Siegel created the popular sex column *Intelligent Lust* for Psychology Today magazine, which is now featured in this collection as well as in *Psychology Tomorrow Magazine*, for which he is Editor-in-Chief. It also appears regularly throughout the Middle East in *FitNStyle* magazine.

Galen Fous, MTP

Over the last 14 years, Galen has worked with hundreds of men, women, and couples seeking support to be honest and empowered about who they are sexually, and healing from the decades of fear, shame and judgments that have held back their authentic desires. He holds a Masters in Transpersonal Psychology from the Institute of Transpersonal Psychology, now known as Sofia University.

His academic and research emphasis is on authentic sexual expression, particularly on what he calls Fetish-sexuality. Galen is actively researching and developing a new therapeutic model of sex therapy for individuals and couples seeking to resolve inner conflicts between their authentic desire and the parts of their psyche that resist their healthy expression. His innovative Sex Research Survey, "Discover Your Personal Erotic Myth," has over 1,200 fascinating and revealing responses so far. He presents regularly at a variety of sexuality-related conferences, graduate and undergraduate psychology programs at colleges and universities, and has been interviewed and written for numerous media for his innovative views on conscious sexuality. His popular column, "The Sex Positive Male," appears twice a month on the Good Men

Project, and his work and research has been featured on the *Dr. Jane Greer Show, Condom Monologues, Psychology Tomorrow Magazine,* the *Dr. Gloria Brame Show,* and many others.

Galen has been advocating for sex-positive approaches to understanding the complex nature of sexual desire and has been active publicly in the Sex-Positive, Fetish/Kink, and Conscious Sexuality communities since 1998. He has also studied and practiced a variety of facilitation and counseling processes, including depth and archetypal psychology, shadow/wound-oriented process work, voice dialogue, neo-tantric practices, mindfulness, embodiment and conscious movement arts, ritual dominance and submission, and BDSM. He has been actively involved in the Mankind Project since February of 1999 and has been a Weekend Leader for both Boys to Men ROP Weekends and Inner Mentor/Adolescent Wound training. His private coaching-counseling practice is located in Portland, OR.

Neil McArthur, PhD

Neil is Associate Professor of Philosophy and Associate Director of the Centre for Professional and Applied Ethics at the University of Manitoba. He researches and teaches courses on sexual ethics and on the history of early modern philosophy.

Ben Peck

Born in 1977 in New London, Connecticut, Ben Peck is a former comparative literature major turned licensed attorney, blogger, writer, escort, and porn performer. He attended Columbia University, where he studied German and Russian literature, then obtained a law degree at Loyola University in Chicago. He found practicing law inconsistent with his moral and ethical values, however, and became a sex worker.

Ben escorted extensively for several years beginning in 2010. He also began working as a porn performer that year, charting a new career course. He lives in New York City, where he continues to care for his disabled partner of 15 years, as well as forge ahead with his career in progressive adult entertainment. Peck does not label himself straight, gay, or bisexual, choosing instead to call himself "omnisexual," committed to sexuality in all its beautiful, life-affirming forms.

Michael Picucci, PhD, MAC, SEP

Dr. Picucci brings decades of investigation and experience to his practice of psychotherapy, Focalizing and consulting. His professional expertise spans a wide range of disciplines as a Psychologist, Licensed Psychotherapist, Master Addictions Counselor, Sexologist, Somatic Experiencing Practitioner, as well as an Organizational Consultant.

Recipient of the National Institutes on Health "Outstanding Leadership in Research Award," the last 30 years of Dr. Picucci's exploration in Social Sciences, Organizational Development, and Energy Psychology has focused on addictions, trauma healing, sexuality, and interpersonal and group dynamics. During this time he has been observing and creating rituals for sane, healthy living for individual clients, couples, groups, and organizations.

Alyssa Siegel, MS, LPC

Alyssa Siegel is a Licensed Professional Counselor in Portland, OR. She earned her MS in Counseling and her BA in Psychology and is a member of The Oregon Board of Licensed Professional Counselors, The American Counseling Association, The National Board of Certified Counselors, The National Coalition for Sexual Freedom, and The Society for the Scientific Study of Sexuality.

Alyssa works with individuals and couples and specializes in relationships, sexuality, and women's identity development. Alyssa is also a contributing author to *Your Brain on Sex: How Smarter Sex Can Change Your Life*.

Bill Hayward

Bill Hayward is a photographer, painter, film maker, and performance artist, whose work is inspired by the drama of living forms. To these ends, he explores the human body—its outward appearance and innermost feelings—often entering territories of vulnerability and emotional risk. Bill's work has been exhibited in galleries and performance centers across the United States and Europe.

Bill's most recent book is *Chasing Dragons* (Glitterati, 2015) a stunning visual autobiography, chronicling more than five decades of artistic vision. In this impressive, autobiographical tour de force, Bill presents more than five decades of visual artwork alongside his own personal narrative—his musings on childhood experiences, moments of epiphany, and the fragments of literature that have inspired him along the way. Arranged in five acts, *Chasing Dragons: An Uncommon Memoir in Photographs* traces the evolution of Bill's work—from traditional portraiture to increasingly abstract and altered images, figurative paintings, dance, performance, and film.

Over the years, Bill has turned away from objective, photographic representations, choosing instead to mine the depths of the human psyche, conveying something elemental, even primordial. Often shrouded, spooky, or distorted, these images are evidence that Bill is both a master artist and skilled psychoanalyst. *Chasing Dragons* tells the story of one artist's quest for self-discovery and new modes of expression—inspiring the same spirit in his subjects and all those who encounter his work.

Bill's previous books of photography include *Cat People* (Doubleday, 1978) and *BadBehavior* (Rizzoli, 2000). Bill's film *asphalt, muscle & bone*, a disruptive about risk and the impossibility of love will be released in 2016.

Bill lives and in works in New York City and Montana.

www.ingramcontent.com/pod-product-compliance
Lightning Source LLC
Chambersburg PA
CBHW080054280326
41934CB00014B/3314